Sayings of
E. Stanley Jones

Books and Resources by

E. Stanley Jones

Used in this Compilation

The Christ of the Mount
The Way
Growing Spiritually
In Christ
Victory Through Surrender
A Song of Ascents
The Reconstruction of the Church
Sat Tal Ashram wall mottoes

Sayings of E. Stanley Jones

A Treasury of Wisdom and Wit

Compiled and Edited by
Whitney J. Dough

Foreword by Maxie Dunnam

Providence House Publishers
Franklin, Tennessee

Material for this compilation used by permission of Eunice Jones Mathews, daughter of E. Stanley Jones.

Books by E. Stanley Jones may be obtained from Christian bookstores or by contacting United Christian Ashrams International, 1500 E. Fairview Ave., Montgomery, Alabama 36106-2114 • (205) 262-6400.

Printed in the United States of America

99 98 97 96 95 94 6 5 4 3 2 1

ISBN 1-881576-29-9

Published by
PROVIDENCE HOUSE PUBLISHERS
P.O. Box 158
Franklin, Tennessee 37065
1-800-321-5692

IN HONOR OF E. STANLEY JONES

THE KEYS OF THE KINGDOM

Louise C. Snow

God gave him the keys of the Kingdom:
"Surrender"—"Accept"—"Believe"—
To be shared with all, the great and the small;
With any who would receive.

He spoke forth the keys of the Kingdom
As the Spirit bade him do,
While he walked The Way in his earthly stay.
His words and his life rang true.

He held out the keys of the Kingdom
For a homesick soul to see,
And the Promised Land was within his hand—
He spoke with authority.

How he used the keys of the Kingdom
To nurture a newborn soul!
And new life became, in Jesus' Name,
Exciting—fulfilling—whole!

He left us the keys of the Kingdom
That the Word once more might be
Made flesh in us all who will heed the call
To live in eternity.

When we take the keys of the Kingdom
To disciple our hearts each day,
Heed the Master's call to surrender all,
Jesus is Lord of The Way!

—Used by permission

Editor's note: Louise C. Snow was led to surrender her life to the unchanging Christ and His unshakable Kingdom by the missionary-evangelist, E. Stanley Jones. Snow is a United Methodist Christian living in Los Angeles, California, and is the acknowledged poet-laureate of the Christian Ashram movement.

Contents

Foreword

Each generation yields a small number of Christian leaders whose spiritual gifts and work demonstrate an enduring quality that transcends their own era. E. Stanley Jones was such a person. His tireless effort in advancing the Gospel of Jesus Christ was without bounds; his ministry incorporated the entire spectrum of humanity—international, inter-racial, inter-denominational, inter-generational; his words and ideas spoke powerfully then, just as they do today.

The remarkable legacy of this humble Christian missionary continues in such tangible ways as the world-wide Christian Ashram movement, the E. Stanley Jones School of Evangelism at Asbury Seminary, the twenty-eight books he authored—Jones' gifts, influence, work, and ministry—all accomplishments for God's glory and purpose.

E. Stanley Jones had profound ideas. He saw ahead into a future where terms like "global economy" and "new world order" would be common buzz-words. He understood the transcending and unifying power of Jesus Christ in such a time. The world needs to hear his message now more than ever before.

My commendation of his work is very personal. There is a sense in which he saved my life for the ministry. I was the organizing pastor of a rapidly growing congregation in Mississippi in the early sixties. The civil rights movement was boiling. Despite every sign of "success" in the congregation, my commitment to Christian love translated into justice and human rights was a constant source of tension. I began to wonder if the Gospel was making any difference at a crucial time that mattered most. I flirted with "throwing in the towel." It was an especially low time in my life.

Then came an invitation to attend a Christian Ashram led by Brother Stanley. It was God's perfect timing. I had read his books and a prayer group of which I was a part was then using his book *In Christ*. So I accepted the invitation. That week changed my life significantly and completely altered the direction of my ministry.

I later had the opportunity of traveling with Brother Stanley in Christian Ashrams in Scandinavia—my first introduction to international ministry. His life, his preaching, his writing have a continuing influence on my life.

For all these reasons I commend the SAYINGS OF E. STANLEY JONES. Here is a well-organized collection of many memorable statements Jones made from a broad range of topics. His joyful outlook is a lesson for each of us as we struggle for faithfulness in this complex day and time.

Pastor and laity alike will gain insight, but more important, they will experience the risen Christ through the inspiration of the man, E. Stanley Jones. I pray, that through this resource, you will discover what Brother Stanley communicated so transparently and powerfully: "Christ in you, the hope of glory."

Maxie Dunnam, President
Asbury Theological Seminary
Wilmore, Kentucky

Preface

Oxford University graduate and ordained Anglican clergyman, Charles Wesley, met a layman, an uneducated mechanic, of whom he said: "He knows nothing but Christ, and yet, by knowing Him, knows and discerns all things!" Wesley was so amazed, so mesmerized, that he went home with the man to seek to find Christ for himself and was led to spiritual conversion through the witness of this layman (Mr. Bray) and the man's sister (Mrs. Turner).

That is one of my favorite stories out of the life of Charles Wesley. It is a story which, I believe, E. Stanley Jones would also appreciate because it demonstrates seven great experiences which Jones emphasized in his own ministry.

1. The power in the life of a Christian witness (the layman and his sister).
2. The remarkable understanding of God and the meanings of life given to those who know Christ (the laypersons).
3. The necessity of spiritual conversion even for those of high moral and educational fitness (Wesley).
4. The poor in spirit (Wesley) are humble enough to receive and do find the Kingdom (Matt. 5:3).
5. The laity play a key role in the ministry of Christ (Mr. Bray and Mrs. Turner).
6. The Word was not just verbal, it was vital; it produced a changed life (Wesley).

7. Evangelists (the layman and his sister) brought to spiritual rebirth another person (Wesley) who in turn became an evangelist. Evangelists produce evangelists.

As I compiled these sayings of Brother Stanley (from seven of his twenty-eight books and the Sat Tal Ashram wall mottoes) I was reminded that E. Stanley Jones, totally immersed in his walk with Christ, had answers to the most profound questions of life. These *sayings* show the way to total personal fulfillment. Therefore, you are holding in your hands a priceless treasure. Brother Stanley lifted up truths vitally needed but often obscured in our culture and even in the church. Our world desperately needs what this man had to say.

The format of using *sayings* (pertinent little epigrams or short statements) will heighten the vividness of truths presented. Epigrams can be called "sermon starters." Most of them contain *seed truths* which suggest deeper explorations of the subject. There is enough seed material within these pages to fuel a lifetime of preaching. Also, using the epigrams in sermons will add sparkle to the message.

In these *sayings* you will discover important themes such as: a moral universe which always has the last word; the Kingdom of God, written not only in the Bible but into the nature of reality and humankind; the need for conversion; the centrality of self surrender; the Holy Spirit; the believer's birthright and cleanser of the self-conscious; victorious living; and many others.

I strongly suggest that for wider understanding you turn to the context passages from which the *sayings* are lifted.

May your reading of these *sayings* be very fruitful.

Whitney J. Dough
Compiler and Editor

ACKNOWLEDGMENTS

To my dear friend, Charles Kinder, whose timely quotes of Stanley Jones prompted the beginnings of this book;

To my beautiful wife, Kathy, for the diligent proof-reading, and to neighborly proof-readers, Louis and Jean Brooks, Betsy Wood, and Dan and Fran McElheny;

To the gifted poet, Louise Snow, for her insightful remembrance of Stanley Jones;

To the great evangelical leader, Maxie Dunnam, for contributing the foreword;

To Bill Pickard, General Secretary of United Christian Ashrams, for biographical material on our writer;

To Eunice Jones Mathews and Bishop James Mathews for permission to glean Stanley Jones' books for this publication;

To Andrew Miller of Providence House Publishers, with his expert staff, for advice, kindly encouragement, and technical assistance;

And finally, thank you to Stanley Jones, himself, for his delightful sense of humor. He told me with a chuckle, "A woman said, 'Brother Stanley, your books are the best cure for insomnia I have ever found!' "

Sayings of
E. Stanley Jones

E. Stanley Jones
1884–1973

Introduction

Biographical Note on E. Stanley Jones

For more than half a century, Dr. E. Stanley Jones proclaimed the Gospel of Christ, and applied it to men's personal, social, national, and international problems as they arose on every continent and among all cultures. He was probably the world's best-known and longest-tested Christian missionary and evangelist. He moved among statesmen and among leaders without portfolios, as counselor, friend, and worker for peace and goodwill. He helped hundreds of thousands, from village outcasts in India to molders of public opinion in America, Japan, Europe, and India.

In addition, he initiated and helped support institutions and movements on five continents—institutions and movements that have aided many thousands to achieve better lives religiously, socially, and medically. The proceeds from his Spiritual Life Missions and speaking engagements in America, as well as the royalties of his twenty eight books—most of them best sellers—were devoted wholly to these enterprises and causes.

E. Stanley Jones was born in Baltimore, Maryland, January 3, 1884. He was educated in Baltimore schools and studied law at City College before being graduated form Asbury College, Wilmore, Kentucky, in 1906. He was on the faculty of Asbury College when he was called to missionary service in India in 1907 under the Board of Missions of the Methodist Episcopal Church.

He began his work among the members of the very low castes and the outcasts. He did not attack Hinduism, Buddhism, Islam, or any Indian religion. He presented the Gospel of Jesus Christ, disentangled from western systems and cultures, and their sometimes non-Christian expressions. "The way of Jesus should be—but often isn't—the way of Christianity," he said. "Western civilization is only partly Christianized."

Brother Stanley, as he was familiarly called by thousands of people, attracted wide attention among the high castes, the students, and the intelligentsia. He was invited to speak at ancient universities and before learned societies. Soon he was set aside by his church to interpret the Christian Gospel especially to educated men and women. In 1919, with foresight and great-heartiness, the Board of Missions of the Methodist Episcopal Church offered him the wide-ranging role of "Evangelist-at-large" to India and to wherever else he might feel led, which subsequently proved to be to the far corners of the earth.

Jones conducted great mass meetings in leading Indian cities. At one such meeting, their leader said, "We may not agree with what Dr. Jones is saying, but we can certainly all try to be like Jesus Christ." He inaugurated *round table conferences* at which Christian and non-Christian sat down as equals to study the basic beliefs that motivate persons. Thirty years before the United Nations came into being, he proposed a Round Table of Nations.

In 1925, while home on furlough, he wrote a report of his years of service—what he had taught and what he had learned in India. It was published in a book titled, *The Christ of the Indian Road* and became a best seller. Other books followed and certain books or single chapters became required reading in various theological seminaries or in degree courses at government colleges in parts of the world. They have been read around jungle fires, studied by armies and governments, quoted in parliaments, and banned and burned by Communists.

In 1928, Stanley Jones was elected a bishop by the General Conference of the Methodist Episcopal Church. However, he felt God had called him to the work of an evangelist and resigned on the eve of his consecration in order to continue his work as a missionary and evangelist. His work became interdenominational and world wide. He held before men the fact of God's reconciliation to mankind through Jesus on the cross. He made Christ visible as the Universal Son of Man who had come for all people. This opening up of nations receiving Christ within their own framework marked a new approach in missions. It came to be known as *indiginization*. He helped to reestablish the Indian *Ashram* (or forest retreat) as a means of drawing men and women together for days at a time to study in depth their own spiritual natures and quest, and what the different faiths offered individuals. Some came to refute the Christian Gospel or extol their own or to accept Christ's way of life. These confrontations of person with person and religion with religion greatly influenced the thought life of India's leaders and the views and activities of its ancient faiths.

Then in 1930, along with a British missionary and Indian pastor and using the sound Christian missionary principle of indiginization, Dr. Jones reconstituted the *Ashram* with Christian disciplines. This institution became known as the *Christian Ashram.* Stranded in the United States during World War II because the only overseas travel allowed was for the military, with his family in India, he transplanted the Christian Ashram to the United States and Canada where it has become a strong spiritual growth ministry.

Stanley Jones went to earth's trouble spots helping to promote international understanding. "Peace", he said, "is a by-product of conditions out of which peace naturally comes . . . If reconciliation is God's chief business, it is ours . . . between man and God, between man and himself and between man and man." His efforts in Burma, Korea, the Belgian Congo, between China and Japan, and between Japan and the United States, to mention only a few, received wide attention. In the months prior to December 7, 1941, he was a constant confidant of Franklin D. Roosevelt and Japanese leaders trying to avert war. In Africa he was called the *Reconcilor.* On his first visit after the war, Japan hailed him with banners saying "Welcome to the Apostle of Peace." He also won the esteem of all India. Men in the old British colony and in the new Indian nation, which came into existence after World War II, counseled with him. His influence had no small share in establishing religious freedom in the new constitution of India.

Dr. Jones became a friend of Mahatma Gandhi and wrote an appreciative biography of Gandhi. Martin Luther King told the daughter of Stanley Jones, Eunice Jones Mathews, that it was reading her father's biography of Gandhi that convinced him to adopt the strict non-violent method in the civil rights struggle. The sons and grandsons of Gandhi remain close friends of the Mathews (Bishop and Mrs. James K. Mathews). For many years, Stanley Jones spent six months in North America, conducting city-wide evangelistic missions, Christian Ashrams, and other spiritual life missions, and the other six months overseas. He preached and held Christian Ashrams in almost every country of the world.

In India he supported students of the Mar Thoma Church preparing for the ministry, students at Leonard Theological Seminary, Indian students studying in America, and itinerating evangelists and Christian workers in rural areas. He subsidized schools for lay leaders, provided "Church extension gifts" to build churches and schools in Indian villages and cities. He had a strong influence in preventing the spread of Communism in India. One of his books is titled *Christ's Alternative to Communism.* He founded, developed, and supported Sat Tal, a full-time ecumenical Christian Ashram as a spiritual center for India, Europe, and America.

In 1947 in the United States, he launched the Crusade for a Federal Union of Churches. He conducted mass meetings from coast to coast and spoke in almost five hundred cities, towns, and churches. He advocated a system though which denominations could unite as they were, each preserving its own distinctive emphasis and heritage, but accepting one another and working together in a kind of federal union patterned after the United State's system of federal union.

In 1950, Dr. Jones provided funds for India's first Christian Psychiatric center and clinic, the now noted Nur Manzil Psychiatric Center and Medical Unit at Lucknow. The staff includes specialists from India, Asia, Africa, Europe, and America who have given up lucrative practices to serve in this Christian institution which serves thousands of patients.

In 1959, E. Stanley Jones was named "Missionary Extraordinary" by the Methodist missionary publication *World Outlook.* A well-known Bishop described him as "the greatest Christian missionary since Saint Paul." He traveled among the peoples of the earth, speaking three or more times daily. A heavy correspondence, writing a book every other year and constant personal counseling completed a program that went on "'round the clock, 'round the year and 'round the world"—a miracle of physical achievement. The years did not weary him, for he was blessed with physical stamina, mental vigor, and God's grace to sustain him in the rugged schedule he imposed upon himself.

In December of 1971, at the age of eighty-eight, while leading the

Oklahoma Christian Ashram, Brother Stanley suffered a stroke that seriously impaired him physically but not mentally and spiritually. He was severely impaired in his speech, but dictated into a tape recorder his last book *The Divine Yes* and in June of 1972 gave moving messages from his wheel chair at the First Christian Ashram World Congress in Jerusalem. He died January 25, 1973, in his beloved India. Indeed, E. Stanley Jones was truly a "Missionary Extraordinary" to the twentieth century!

William M. Pickard
General Secretary
United Christian Ashram International

Favorite Scriptures of E. Stanley Jones

These are the verses E. Stanley Jones especially loved to quote and expound. Many of the *sayings* come from these favorite scriptures.

Hebrews 12:28— ***"... we are receiving a Kingdom which cannot be shaken."***
Hebrews 13:8— ***"Jesus Christ, the same yesterday and today and forever."***

The Unshakable Kingdom and the Unchanging Person. Christ and His Kingdom are the same. Jesus used the terms "for My sake" and "for the Kingdom's sake" interchangeably.

Revelation 7:17— ***"... the Lamb at the center of the Throne."***

Self-giving love is at the heart of the universe, has the last word.

John 1:14— ***"The Word became flesh...."***

Not verbal, but vital. The spiritual and the material are joined and everything is sacred.

Colossians 1:16— ***"All things were made by Him [Christ] and for Him."***

Everything has the touch of Christ upon it. We are created to be Christian, every fiber, every tissue, and violating His way brings disaster. We are allergic to sin.

2 Corinthians 5:19— ***"God was in Christ reconciling the world to Himself, and He has committed to us the ministry of reconciliation."***

Every Christian, especially the laity, is to carry the message of reconciliation, the cross, and be an evangelist.

Sayings of E. Stanley Jones

Anger

A man put on the back of his car a sign which read: "Honk away, it's your ulcer."

—*Growing Spiritually*

The Christian way is not only sanctity; it is sanity.

—*The Way*

We hate ourselves for hating.

—*Growing Spiritually*

The sins of omission and commission are bad, but the worst sins are those of disposition.

—*The Way*

You cannot abuse another without abusing yourself.

—*Growing Spiritually*

Wrong attitudes toward people produce wrong effects in the body.

—*Growing Spiritually*

Men cannot get along with each other because they cannot get along with themselves, and they cannot get along with themselves because they cannot get along with God.

—*The Way*

If in the heat of an impulse you write a stinging letter, don't send it. Sleep over it, and see how it looks the next morning when your passion has subsided and you enter the stage of consideration. You'll probably tear it up. If not, it will probably tear you up with remorse and repentance.

—*Growing Spiritually*

I have only one remedy, for I find only one disease—self at the center, self trying to be God.

—*Victory Through Surrender*

ASTROLOGY

Stargazing for life guidance is silly, and worse, it is a blight on any civilization that adopts it.

—*The Reconstruction of the Church*

When people lose the guidance of God, they will turn to anything for guidance.

—*In Christ*

To take your eyes off the cross and put them on the stars or to spend your time in trying to peep beyond the veil of death, is to substitute the purposely concealed for the purposely revealed.

—*In Christ*

One of the things that strikes me as strange when I come back from the East where astrology has reigned and where they are gradually throwing it off as an outworn superstition, is finding the newspapers of America printing daily horoscopes.

—*In Christ*

It is a sign of moral decay. If one has lost his nerve to make moral judgments and decisions, he turns to the stars and lets them decide for him.

—*The Reconstruction of the Church*

The Greek mind was creative until the dead hand of astrology took over and ruined it. The Hindu mind is a very acute mind and deeply philosophical, but its feet are not on earth, for it is gazing at the stars for guidance.

—*The Reconstruction of the Church*

Nothing would paralyze a civilization quicker than for its citizens to abandon the responsibility of moral and spiritual choice in favor of letting the stars decide.

—*In Christ*

Perpetuation of this superstition by newspapers shows an incredible moral and spiritual shallowness . . . materialism of the grossest kind.

—*In Christ*

BIBLE

The Word was not made printer's ink. The Word was made flesh, not a page but a Person.

—*The Way*

No person can be spiritual who is not scriptural. If there is dust on your Bible, there is dust on your experience of Christ.

—*In Christ*

When I was first converted I used to wander out in the fields with my New Testament, and I found my self pressing my lips upon a specially luminous passage. I met the Word in the word.

—*Song of Ascents*

In order for the Spirit to guide us through the Word, we must be soaked in that Word.

—*Growing Spiritually*

Let God speak to you through His Word, before you speak to Him through your words.

—*The Way*

There are thirty-three thousand promises in the Scriptures, and Jesus is the Yes to every one of them.

—*In Christ*

What liberty it brings if we put our lives under the guidance of the Book and let it speak to our present conditions! God must have gone into this Word, for God comes out of it.

—*Growing Spiritually*

If you settle the question of who wrote the Pentateuch, or the two Isaiahs, you've settled textual questions; but if you settle who Jesus Christ is, you've settled practically all the questions in heaven and on earth.

—*Song of Ascents*

You don't have to decide anything personally when you try to decide who wrote the Pentateuch, but you have to decide something personally when you face Jesus . . . He is the point of decision.

—*Song of Ascents*

While I am not a fundamentalist or a modernist, only a Christian-in-the-making, I do love this Book, for these words take me beyond the words to the Word.

—*Song of Ascents*

If we are to be spiritual, we have to be scriptural. Neglect the Scriptures and you neglect to grow, to be alive.

—*Song of Ascents*

As I understand it the Christian faith in its New Testament form asks nothing less and nothing more than self-surrender to God.

—*Victory Through Surrender*

We are the only Bible some people will read.

—In Christ

BOREDOM

If you are bored with your work, change your job or change your attitude. Do everything for the love of God.

—The Way

BUSINESS

Unless there is a basis of morality in the community, then business is impossible.

—The Way

The Christian way is the Way to run a business.

—The Reconstruction of the Church

Dishonesty puts sand in the internal and external machinery of life.

—Growing Spiritually

A civilization saves or damns its soul by the way it wins its bread.

—The Way

The Sermon on the Mount of yesterday is the Sermon for the Mart today.

—The Way

CHRIST, JESUS LORD

Jesus is Lord.

—Sat Tal Ashram wall mottoes

My creed and my song are one—my creed, "Jesus is Lord"; my song, "Jesus is Lord!" I'm in Him and He is in me! Hallelujah!

—In Christ

A nail-pierced hand holds the sceptre of the universe, and my knees bend before Him.

—Victory Through Surrender

Jesus is Lord in every situation He is in . . . And He is in every situation.

—Song of Ascents

We must be fixed to something universal and timeless.

—The Reconstruction of the Church

Jesus is Lord in three directions: Lord of the past, Lord of the present, Lord of the future.

—Song of Ascents

The God-is-dead theologians are not theologians but morticians, and their "theology" is deomortology.

—The Reconstruction of the Church

I don't know what the future holds, but I know Who holds the future.

—*In Christ*

The whole of religion in general and Christianity in particular is reduced to three words: "Jesus is Lord."

—*Song of Ascents*

Christianity: here then, was a movement founded on His life, His teaching, His death, His resurrection, His coming by the Holy Spirit, His program of the Kingdom for individual and collective redemption, a movement whose Author is at the right hand of power, has "all authority!"

I'm not interested in "apostolic succession" for the terminus of my faith is not the apostles, but Jesus Christ.

—*In Christ*

Christ, Jesus Person of

You find God when you find Jesus. The more you know of Jesus the more you know of God.

—*In Christ*

It is a liberating experience to find one's faith becoming simplified and centered in a Person.

—*The Christ of the Mount*

How could twelve ignorant fishermen create a character like Jesus?

—*Song of Ascents*

Christianity is Christ.

—*Song of Ascents*

God's method is a Man.

—*The Christ of the Mount*

I belong to the timeless and the deathless: I belong to Jesus Christ.

—*Song of Ascents*

God's idea about Himself is Christ.

—*The Way*

Jesus is the simplification of God. All great discoveries are simplifications. Thought moves from the complicated to the simple.

—*The Christ of the Mount*

Jesus is the self-revelation of God.

—*Song of Ascents*

You cannot say God until you first say Jesus.

—*Song of Ascents*

If this is the Heart of the universe, then He can have my heart.

—The Christ of the Mount

Jesus is not merely the founder of our faith; He is the foundation.

—Song of Ascents

Jesus is not a Third Person standing between me and God. Rather He is God projected to me, God become available. He is mediator in the sense that He mediates God to me, for when I take hold of Him I take hold of the very self of God.

—The Christ of the Mount

Wherever life gets into touch with Him, really into touch with Him, it is lifted, changed, saved.

—The Way

Bring everything to Jesus. Don't struggle with your problems, don't push them into the subconscious mind, don't go from person to person for solution, but bring everything , especially your self and its problems to Jesus.

—Song of Ascents

I shall begin with the Person and work from Him down to my problems.

—The Way

You cannot love Christ unless you surrender to Christ.

—Victory Through Surrender

I can do very little alone; we can do anything together.

—The Way

The most wonderful thing about life is this: You are subjected to the most absolutely stimulating moral and spiritual and intellectual and physical force in the universe, namely, the Spirit of Christ.

—Growing Spiritually

Sermon on the Mount: This is not a sermon—it is a portrait of Jesus Himself, and of the Father, and of the man-to-be.

—The Christ of the Mount

Go beyond your sins, beyond the institution, beyond the principles to the Person. Then religion will be to you a long falling in love!

—The Way

It took an emotional upheaval to carry me across from a self-preoccupied life to a Christ-preoccupied life . . . I looked into his face and was forever spoiled for anything unlike Him.

—Song of Ascents

Mahatma Gandi took the principles of Christianity, but missed the Person—Christ. Hence he sees "through a glass darkly."

—*The Way*

You are not a Christian because you don't do this, that, or the other. You are a Christian when life is centered in Christ and not in yourself.

—*The Way*

The Talmud held treasures amid much rubbish. But Jesus hits the essential and always the essential. His was the sifted mind. He was never misled by a subordinate issue, never took a bypath, and never missed the point.

—*The Christ of the Mount*

Christianity is moonlight, secondhand, built up through the centuries; Christ is sunlight, firsthand, not built up through the centuries, but revealed from eternity—the revelation of the meaning of God and man and life.

—*The Reconstruction of the Church*

Jesus is God's latchstring hung so low that even a child can reach it and open the door—to everything!

—*Growing Spiritually*

I brought to them the Word—Christ.

—*The Way*

Every departure from Him (Jesus) in thought or emphasis brings decay.

—*The Reconstruction of the Church*

Everything that Jesus said is founded upon the bedrock of the moral and spiritual facts of the universe.

—*The Christ of the Mount*

I don't have to defend Jesus. I have to present Him, and He is His own defense.

—*Song of Ascents*

Legend says that where Jesus walked, flowers sprang up in His footprints. That is legend, but the moral and spiritual of that does happen.

—*Growing Spiritually*

A member of a Unitarian group came to me and said, "Won't you come to our national convention and help us get God back. We are drifting into humanism." That was strange. Unitarianism which concentrated on God was losing Him, and I who concentrated on Jesus had found God.

—*In Christ*

The Christian Ashram would revolve around Jesus Christ.
—*Song of Ascents*

Jesus fits me as a hand fits a glove, as light fits the eye, as love fits the heart, as beauty fits the aesthetic nature. When we find Him we find ourselves.
—*Song of Ascents*

All the ideas of the Christian faith are guaranteed by the fact of Christ. They have taken shoes and walked. We not only hear them—we see them. And what we see are so good, so beautiful, so true that they become the Good, the Beautiful, and the True. His ways become the Way, His truths become the Truth, and His life becomes the Life.
—*Song of Ascents*

"Thou shalt call His name Jesus." That one Name is the rock upon which the future civilization of the world will be built—or shattered. In either case it is rock!
—*The Christ of the Mount*

Life equals food, says the biochemist. Life equals emotion, says the sensualist. Life equals money, says the materialist. Life equals Christ, says the Christian.
—*The Way*

A little Italian boy said, "Jesus is the best photograph that God ever took." The writer of Hebrews says He is "the express image of His person," an exact likeness of God.
—*The Way*

The name of Jesus is not merely written into Western civilization—it is plowed in. More books have been written about Jesus than about any hundred others. And wherever they have listened, listened and obeyed, to that degree life has been enobled, purified, and regenerated.
—*The Reconstruction of the Church*

The only possible way that God could perfectly reveal Himself is through a perfect Person.
—*Song of Ascents*

Christ is my reward.
—*Song of Ascents*

CHRIST, JESUS SAVIOR/REDEEMER

He confronts me with an offer of salvation that only God can offer. So instead of putting my hand on His shoulder, I find myself at His feet.
—*The Christ of the Mount*

Unless you surrender to the person of Jesus, you do not know the power of Jesus.

—*Victory Through Surrender*

He lifts me; therefore I uplift Him.

—*In Christ*

He is like me, therefore my Example; He is unlike me, therefore my Redeemer.

—*The Christ of the Mount*

The fact of the living Christ is the best corroborated fact in history; for in every clime, in every age, among all peoples the experience is the same: Christ—alive, redeeming, joy-producing, love-creating—moves straight into the hearts of people everywhere as a present Fact. We not merely remember Jesus; we realize Him!

—*The Way*

Salvation is in Christ and not in the system built up around Him.

—*In Christ*

In Christ life makes sense. Our sums are all adding up to the right answers.

—*Growing Spiritually*

Everything Jesus touches He enriches.

—*In Christ*

Fix in mind that no man, no institution, no creed, no denomination, no group, no rite, no ceremony can be invested with saving qualities without disappointment or letdown. All of these have to be saved.

—*The Way*

I didn't find God— He found me. I turned around in repentance and faith, and I was in His arms.

—*Song of Ascents*

This is the central weakness of organized Christianity—it preaches salvation through Christ, but not salvation in Christ.

—*In Christ*

I call Him Savior because He saves me now.

—*Song of Ascents*

There is only one issue left to modern man; it is increasingly Christ or nothing. All other alternatives are being eliminated.

—*In Christ*

The "Gentile dogs" have become the leaders of civilization. At the basis of that leadership is the stimulus of Jesus Christ. He makes the nobodies into somebodies, the down-and-outs into up-and-on-tops.

—*In Christ*

The broken pieces of our life mistakes can be gathered up and built into a temple of God. He redeems the past as well as cleanses it.

—*Song of Ascents*

You are not saved from sin by becoming obsessed with it. You must become obsessed with the Savior. It is not humility to be always talking about how sinful you are after redemption; it is a slur on the Redeemer.

—*Growing Spiritually*

Jesus is God available.

—*Song of Ascents*

Fifty-nine years ago I looked into His eyes and saw forgiveness there, and I've never gotten over the spell of it.

—*In Christ*

The Sermon on the Mount cannot be lived apart from the Savior of the Mount.

—*The Christ of the Mount*

CHRIST, JESUS, UNIVERSALITY OF

He is the Christ of the Beginnings and the Christ of the Final Word.

—*The Christ of the Mount*

Jesus is at home in every race, in every land.

—*In Christ*

Wherever we go in life we meet Christ.

—*The Way*

Jesus is nowhere out of place.

—*Sal Tal Ashram wall mottoes*

The immediate availability of Jesus to human need is the most precious fact in life.

—*In Christ*

The Christian faith is the good news of the one universal God, revealed in the universal Man, and presenting the universal Kingdom, founded on universal principles, and offered to universal man.

—*The Reconstruction of the Church*

Everywhere is home to me, for Christ is everywhere and He is my Home.

—*Growing Spiritually*

If you want to be universal and valid today: be Christian.

—*The Reconstruction of the Church*

One blood for us—the Blood of Christ. One blood in us—the blood of humanity.

—*The Way*

Every single thing Jesus was interested in and everything He insisted upon is now becoming and will increasingly become the interest of humanity; that is, if humanity is to survive.

—*The Reconstruction of the Church*

The more Christian you are, the more universal you are. You are at home in everything, everywhere except one thing—evil.

—*The Way*

He belonged to everybody because he belonged to Christ. The Christian is pro-everybody, he is only anti-evil.

—*The Way*

There isn't a situation on earth, for the individual, for society, where the Christian thing is not the right thing.

—*The Way*

CHRISTLIKENESS

The highest adjective descriptive of character in any language is the adjective Christlike.

—*Victory Through Surrender*

A girl, recently in the Kingdom, said: "I like the person I'm becoming."

—*Song of Ascents*

The Holy Spirit produces Christlike persons.

—*Song of Ascents*

Nothing is more beautiful than a truly Christian person.

—*In Christ*

The purpose of the whole is nothing less than being changed into His likeness. How tawdry this goal makes the ordinary goals seem—to get to heaven, to escape hell, to be happy, to be healthy, to be successful.

—*In Christ*

Humans are invited to be like God in self-surrender.

—*Victory Through Surrender*

No thorns in the flesh can really hurt me, for I have none in my heart to impair me.

—*Growing Spiritually*

Today I shall treat everybody as Christ treats me.

—*The Way*

He became like us that we might become like Him.

—*Song of Ascents*

I, who have been made in the image of sin, am now being made in the image of the Savior.

—*Song of Ascents*

In the New Testament, apart from the book of Revelation, heaven is spoken of twelve times as a place to which men go hereafter. But not once is it spoken of as the goal of life. Perfection is mentioned thirty-three times and always as the goal of life.

—*Growing Spiritually*

When I think of goodness I think of Jesus of Nazareth.

—*Song of Ascents*

Clemenceau said, "When a Christian decides to live his Christianity, then a real revolution begins.

—*The Way*

The only way to avenge yourself is not to become like the wrongdoer.

—*The Christ of the Mount*

Jesus is the way to act for everybody, everywhere. God could not do an unChristlike thing and still be God. He would violate His own nature.

—*In Christ*

We are to be salt before we can be light. . . . Many of us would like to be light, but we are unwilling to work like salt, unseen, unnoticed, unapplauded.

—*The Christ of the Mount*

The highest kind of character is that which spontaneously takes the right attitudes.

—*The Way*

I have seen Him and shall never be satisfied until I shall wake in His likeness. He has set me afire to be like Him.

—*In Christ*

In any situation look at Jesus and do the most Christlike thing you know, and you will never go wrong.

—*The Way*

John Foster Dulles saw that you couldn't make an international conference work without the Christian spirit. So he who was skeptical became a convinced and committed Christian, pushed into it by the very pressures of life.

—*The Way*

Jesus did not come merely to disclose God's character. He came to make it possible to be remade in the likeness of that character.

—*Song of Ascents*

Let not this group SEEK the answer but BE the answer.

—*Sat Tal Ashram wall mottoes*

The Christian always wins if he remains Christian.

—*Song of Ascents*

Church, Functioning of

With all its faults, the Church is the best serving institution on earth. It has many critics but no rivals in the work of human redemption. It has filled the earth with schools, hospitals, orphanages, blind and leper asylums, churches—everything to lift the soul of the race to higher levels.

—*The Way*

If you are not in the Church, get in. If you are marginally in, get into the center.

—*The Way*

Everyone needs a group fellowship in which the group is a conspiracy of love to make and keep each member the best person he is capable of being. If anyone hasn't such a group fellowship, he should find or create one; life demands it.

—*Song of Ascents*

Let the Church be organized love—to all.

—*The Way*

Group Fellowship: The group becomes the emery paper by which the rough edges of conduct and attitude are smoothed out in our characters. But after the smoothing by emery the group can then become the burnishing powder by which we are polished to shine for His glory.

—*Growing Spiritually*

Let the foundation be Christ, let the superstructure be Christian, and then let life do its worst or its best. It stands.

—*The Christ of the Mount*

Completely committed to Christ and unbreakably committed to each other in abiding fellowship.

—*Sat Tal Ashram wall mottoes*

A woman in Korea knocked at the door of a church and said: "Is this the place where they mend broken hearts?"

—*Song of Ascents*

Yes, we specialize in mending broken hearts, broken homes, broken relationships, broken bodies, and broken hopes. This is our chief business—all else is secondary. The chief business of the church is redemption—the mending of broken everything.

—*The Reconstruction of the Church*

No other institution or movement specializes on the person of Jesus Christ.

—The Reconstruction of the Church

If you wipe out the Church today, you would have to put something in its place tomorrow, for it is rooted in the necessities of human living.

—The Way

Centered in Christ we gather; centered in anything else, we scatter.

—The Reconstruction of the Church

What are the values which the church is guarding? I would name six: (1) the Kingdom of God; (2) the person of Jesus Christ; (3) the possibility of a new birth in this birth; (4) the power of the Holy Spirit within, enabling men to live out dynamically this new life in the midst of society; (5) a fellowship of believers in which these four values can be cultivated and a nucleus from which they can be propogated . . . the church; (6) service to all as the only method of greatness for all.

—The Reconstruction of the Church

The listening church shall have fresh news from God.

—The Reconstruction of the Church

Moise Tshombe, when he was Prime Minister of the Congo, said to me, "Apart from the Christian church I see no hope for Africa. Where the church is strong, we have few or no problems; where the church is weak or absent, we have nothing but problems."

—Song of Ascents

To the degree the church listens to God and obeys, the people will listen to the church and will obey its Lord.

—The Reconstruction of the Church

The church contains the best life of the Kingdom, but it is not the Kingdom.

—Song of Ascents

There is no real promise of hope from any direction except the church of Jesus Christ, if that church is truly Christian.

—The Reconstruction of the Church

Not dogmatism, but demonstration.

—Growing Spiritually

No minister can help his people if he isn't delivered from the people to whom he is sent. His herd instinct must be fastened on the Kingdom of God as the supreme loyalty.

—The Way

Be a member of this group or that denomination, but do not belong to it—belong to Christ. The group or denomination belongs to you; you do not belong to it.

—*The Way*

India has gone through three stages in her response to the Christian faith: (1) It isn't true. (2) It isn't new. (3) It isn't you!

—*Song of Ascents*

When the Church listens to the Holy Spirit, it becomes fruitful. New movements are born.

—*The Way*

Sunday Morning Service: The center of the life of the church of today, both liberal and conservative, is the Sunday morning service. Around that Sunday morning service the life of the church revolves. Take that out and there isn't much left. The biggest crowd assembles for it, the greatest preparation goes into it, the greatest expectancy centers there. If anything happens, it happens there. For this is the one and only contact the church has with the majority of its members, and it is the one and only contact the majority of the members have with the church. It is the nerve center of the church. If any message or life impulses go out into the body of the church, it goes out from there.

—*The Reconstruction of the Church*

If the church majors on minors, it will be a minor issue in society—sidelined.

—*The Reconstruction of the Church*

The church would be a filling station and a checkup station for a long and hard week's run for the laity.

—*The Reconstruction of the Church*

The church of today must regain that sense of corporateness, of being a society that has meaning for all life, that when men belong to it they belong to something that has present and ultimate meanings.

—*The Way*

Speaking in tongues: It will divide any group it comes into.

—*Song of Ascents*

It is comparatively easy and cheap to praise God, for in doing so we offer Him our words, but in listening we offer Him ourselves. . . . So praising God is cheap and verbal—listening to God is expensive—and vital.

—*In Christ*

Modern man wants to know "Is the way of Christ the best?" That and that alone is what modern man is wanting the reconstructed church to answer. If it cannot answer that, it has no answer. And the answer must be not just verbal expression, but also a vital experience.

—*The Reconstruction of the Church*

A judge puts it this way: "Almost all juvenile delinquency comes out of non-Sunday school youth and almost all divorces come out of nonchurchgoing groups."

—*The Reconstruction of the Church*

Among Americans as a whole, there is one divorce in four marriages; among church members, one in fifty; among those who pray and read their Bibles in family prayers, one in five hundred. Evidently exposure to God and Christ in prayer in a family circle, plus fellowship of the church, makes for family stability, a great asset to society.

—*The Reconstruction of the Church*

If the church is pastor-centered, then the output will be rhetoric; if it is laycentered, the output will be action.

—*The Reconstruction of the Church*

He could perform a cermony but he couldn't produce a conversion.

—*The Reconstruction of the Church*

It is better to get ten men to work than to do ten men's work.

—*The Reconstruction of the Church*

Men and women who during the week are molders of opinion, directors of large concerns, directors of destinies are expected to be putty on Sunday, and are supposed to like it. They have little responsibility, hence make little response. . . . They have little to do, hence they do little.

—*The Reconstruction of the Church*

The conservative is a necessary element in human society. Without him we start blank. But without the radical, life stops with the past and we lack progress. The prophet is usually the radical, wanting to apply values to wider ranges of life.

—*The Reconstruction of the Church*

We must go back to the Bible, but we must go forward in listening and obeying "what the Spirit says to the churches" and to your church in particular for today in today's environment.

—*The Reconstruction of the Church*

Many of our churches are vaguely religious, instead of being vitally Christian—and they are growing empty.

—The Reconstruction of the Church

Description of Church Service: An ash-covered coal with a feeble warmth within, trying to fellowship in warm fellowship with other ash-covered coals. There are more ashes than glowing coal, and the meetings are non-expectant—perfunctory. This prayer prayed in such a meeting would not be out of place: "O God, if any spark of divine grace has been kindled in this meeting, water that spark."

—Growing Spiritually

Every person, male or female, who is in Christ is ordained.

—In Christ

One of the greatest of mission fields, if not the greatest, is the church members who are bogged down in their trivialities, producing little or nothing, busy at being busy. . . .

—The Reconstruction of the Church

I wanted the Kingdom of God, wanted reconciliation with my heavenly Father, but took church membership as a substitute.

—Song of Ascents

Rev. 3:16-17—Christ was trying to get inside the church! Self was at the center and Christ was at the door knocking. The center of life needed to be redeemed.

—The Way

Sitting in a church does not make a man a Christian any more than sitting in a hen house makes a man a hen.

—Growing Spiritually

I have spent half my life trying to win men to Christ and the church, and the other half trying to win the church to Christ.

—The Reconstruction of the Church

The fact that the modern church could switch so readily from evangelism as decision to evangelism as dialogue or discussion, and do it without any searching of heart, showed the prevailing church climate. The church is at home in dialogue, it is not at home in decision.

—The Reconstruction of the Church

The church is the mother of my spirit. When I point out its faults, I point out my own.

—The Reconstruction of the Church

The Christian Ashram: a vacation with God.

—Song of Ascents

A leading psychologist said: "That Church of today is like an autumn leaf, dry and dead, but retaining its form and structure." Too sweeping, of course, but with just enough truth in it to make it sting.

—*The Way*

The Church is wonderful as a place of worship and spiritual cultivation, provided you go beyond it to Christ. If your relationship to it makes you stop in self-satisfaction this side of a personal, saving relationship with Him, it is a stumbling block.

—*The Way*

Is it any wonder that the church has had problems through the ages? When it drew up its creeds, the Apostles', the Athanasian, the Nicene, it mentioned the Kingdom of God once in all three of them, and then only marginally, beyond the borders of this life, a heavenly Kingdom. No wonder the Church has stumbled from problem to problem when its supreme value was lost or only marginally held. The church will never get straightened out until it puts the Kingdom where Jesus put it in this prayer—the first consideration and the first allegiance.

—*The Way*

The church's confusion and comparative impotence in this confused and groping age is because it has lost its absolute, the unshakeable Kingdom.

—*The Reconstruction of the Church*

CHURCH, ORGANIZATION OF

A divided church in a divided world lacks moral authority.

—*Song of Ascents*

A high churchman was asked in India if he would allow Jesus to preach in his pulpit if He should come, and the reply was: "No, I'm sorry I couldn't, for He wasn't ordained."

—*In Christ*

The structure of Christian churches is fundamentally unchristian—it is competitive, not cooperative.

—*The Reconstruction of the Church*

I belong not to an apostolic faith, but to a Christian faith. Let me live as one who glances at the apostles and gazes at Christ.

—*In Christ*

The church is not an apostolic church—it is not centered in the apostles, it is centered in Christ.

—*The Reconstruction of the Church*

The missing link in apostolic succession is the link between Christ and the apostles, for there is no link of laying on of His hands. That is fatal to the theory.

—*In Christ*

Our emphasis is not and should not be the ecumenical church.

—*Song of Ascents*

A definition of ordination that would rule out the Founder of the faith shows how far we have wandered from that faith.

—*In Christ*

Any attempt to find greatness through popes and prelates and ecclesiastic position and power is an alien type of power imported into the Christian faith. It is always corrupting, for it is alien to the faith it purports to lead.

—*In Christ*

My inner life has been washed clean of the desire for office and prestige. I have what I want—the open opportunity of being a missionary and evangelist.

—*Song of Ascents*

The attempt to become God is the central sin of religion. It is an attempt to enthrone the self as God.

—*Victory Through Surrender*

There are many politically minded people in religious positions using religion as the frontage to backstage political maneuvering for position, place, power. They are not bad people—they are divided.

—*The Way*

Christianity, the system built up around Christ, is often the enemy, the worst enemy of Christ.

—*The Reconstruction of the Church*

I become like that which I worship.

—*The Way*

Suppose we go out and say, "Repent! for the ecumenical church is at hand!" The world would smile. . . . But when we say, "Repent, the Kingdom of God is at hand," you don't smile.

—*Song of Ascents*

Credentials are not from "authorities," but from the authority of the facts produced, changed lives. They, and they alone, are the only valid religious authority in the future. "By their fruits you shall know them."

—*The Reconstruction of the Church*

The church is a relativism, related to the Absolute, the Kingdom of God.

—*Song of Ascents*

If we try to find our unity in the apostles we will be forever divided. If we find it in Christ we will be forever united.

—*The Reconstruction of the Church*

I ask not for authority but for power—and the power becomes the authority.

—*In Christ*

I'm not interested in apostolic succession—only in Christian succession.

—*In Christ*

The New Testament knows of many churches, but knows of one Church.

—*In Christ*

When a little girl was asked by another little girl to go to a meeting she replied, "I'm sorry I can't go with you. I belong to another abomination." Sometimes denominations become abominations, if they separate us from fellow Christians.

—*In Christ*

Each nation in the League of Nations saved its life, refused to surrender any sovereignty to the union, and lost its life in universal chaos and war.

—*The Way*

The modern idea of many churches, separate, sovereign, independent, is unknown in the New Testament.

—*In Christ*

The open possibility is federal union . . . The name of the united church: "The Church of Jesus Christ in America." This union would be a branch union. . . .

—*The Reconstruction of the Church*
(*See above*, ch. 15: "The Reconstruction of the Church—On What Pattern?" for a complete picture of Dr. Jones' suggestions for a Christian Church united.)

Federal union offers union and freedom in a living blend.

—*Song of Ascents*

The people want union, but they also want to preserve their heritage. If the leaders of church union forget that, they will run up against apparent apathy which is not apathy but silent protest. The people want union but do not want to be herded into uniformity.

—*Song of Ascents*

Federal union expresses the principle on which the universe is built.

—*The Reconstruction of the Church*

Federal union would mean the pooling of our lights.

—*Song of Ascents*

I feel that putting all denominations into one system, a merger, would be impoverishing. A federal union of the churches would bring these diversities into a union without losing the diversities.

—*In Christ*

A union in diversity—a federal union: Jesus Christ, and Jesus Christ alone, is the center of our unity. Everyone who belongs to Christ belongs to every one who belongs to Christ. You do not have to seek for unity. You have it—in Christ. All you have to do is proclaim that unity.

—*Song of Ascents*

The only type of unity in diversity that I know of is Federal Union. Federal Union puts together two apparently contradictory urges—the desire for union with the whole and the desire for local freedom. It puts together union and freedom and thus fulfills our very nature.

—*In Christ*

If the Ashram becomes an end in itself it should end.

—*Song of Ascents*

The ecumenical church is a relativism, related to something higher than itself, the Kingdom of God. To confront relativisms with another relativism is bad strategy and bound to fail.

—*The Reconstruction of the Church*

It is the depravity of institutions and movements that given in the beginning to express life they often end in throttling that very life. Therefore they need constant review, perpetual criticism; a continuous bringing back to original purposes and spirit. The Chrisitian church is no exception. It is the chief illustration of the above.

—*The Reconstruction of the Church*

Conscience

Conscience is a capacity to distinguish between right and wrong, but what it distinguishes as right and wrong is determined largely according to training.

—*The Way*

The Christian cannot turn his conscience over to a group . . . he has direct and primary responsibility to God.

—*Growing Spiritually*

Conscience, therefore, is not a safe guide unless it is trained at the feet of Christ and there taught to approve the Christlike things. Paul says, "My conscience bears me out in the Holy Spirit" (Rom. 9:1).

—*The Way*

Your conscience, in Christ must be trained by the Holy Spirit.

—*In Christ*

CONVERSION
NEW BIRTH FROM ABOVE

At seventeen, going through adolescence, I stumbled across this treasure of conversion, this treasure without which this present age is stumbling and fumbling into moral and spiritual chaos.

—*Song of Ascents*

Every generation needs regeneration—especially this one.

—*The Reconstruction of the Church*

For me the new birth gave birth to everything.

—*Song of Ascents*

John (the Baptist) tried to produce reformation; Jesus produced regeneration.

—*Song of Ascents*

Man is made for conversion, as the duck is made for water, the bird is made for the air, the heart is made for love, the aesthetic nature is made for beauty. When you are converted and find Christ you find yourself, your Homeland.

—*Song of Ascents*

The deepest need of man, East, West, North, and South, is to be converted.

—*Song of Ascents*

This was the most sensible thing I ever did—barring none.

—*Song of Ascents*

Not the regulation of conduct, but a regeneration of character.

—*The Christ of the Mount*

Religious rite, or its absence, is irrelevant; the thing that matters is a new creature, a transformed person.

—*The Reconstruction of the Church*

Moses gave a set of commands; Jesus gave the set of the new character.

—*The Christ of the Mount*

He doesn't begin by changing our deeds; He begins by changing us.

—*In Christ*

I walked up to my chum, Ras, slapped him on the back, and said, "My, what a d— fine day," using the old vocabulary to express my newfound joy. The angels must have smiled and said, "He's trying to say 'Hallelujah' but he doesn't know the language yet. Let him alone; he'll get it."

—*Song of Ascents*

Moral and spiritual new birth, which the builders of modern civilization have rejected, has now become the head of the corner, the supreme necessity of modern life. Our intelligence has outrun our character.

—*The Reconstruction of the Church*

All men are one, their needs are one; all men need conversion regardless of label.

—*Song of Ascents*

We are groping and empty. The modern man stands between two worlds—one dead and the other not born. And he cannot stand this emptiness. That emptiness, according to Jung, is "the central neurosis of our time." Man needs conversion.

—*The Reconstruction of the Church*

No amendment, no attainment.

—*Song of Ascents*

We are called into the new life in many ways, by many means. It doesn't matter how we come, if we end up at His feet—changed.

—*Growing Spiritually*

I know nothing, absolutely nothing so potent, so redeeming, so transforming as the direct and immediate impact of Jesus Christ upon the framework of human nature. It creates miracles of changed character around the world among all classes, among all degrees of culture, among all ages, among both sexes. Jesus is Lord.

—*Song of Ascents*

Our main emphasis is on reconciliation to God, conversion, new birth, self-surrender, receiving the Holy Spirit.

—*Song of Ascents*

Except the Mineral Kingdom be born from above it cannot see the Kingdom of the Plant.

—*The Christ of the Mount*

"I hate you. Where are you?" And are not many winds saying in essence: "If you can't convert me, I'll sue you for breach of promise? Why don't you do what you are called to do, convert us?"

—*The Reconstruction of the Church*

Conversion is a profound change in character and life, followed by an outer change which corresponds to that inner change.

—The Reconstruction of the Church

To be reborn is an open possibility to everybody, everywhere, in any condition, in any circumstances. That is the open door. . . .

—The Reconstruction of the Church

When something happens to us, then something happens through us!

—The Way

It is the business of religion, the chief business, to produce conversion. And when it can no longer do so it has lost its right to be called Christian.

—The Reconstruction of the Church

Two thirds of the people in the churches are a field for evangelism instead of a force for evangelism. I have therefore spent more than half of my life in trying to convert unconverted church members.

—Song of Ascents

I have come to the conclusion that two-thirds of the people in the churches need conversion.

—Song of Ascent

People flock to churches which can and do convert them and desert the churches which cannot.

—The Reconstruction of the Church

Both the "down-and-out" and the "up-and-out" need conversion. . . . Human nature is the most changeable thing on earth.

—The Way

In conversion there is introduced into the soul a new life, the life of the Spirit; you are born of the Spirit.

—The Way

Everything must be brought to the bar of one judgment: does it produce a new creature both in the individual and the corporate life? If so, it stays; if not, out it goes. We must be stripped for action, Christian action, the action that produces the new creature individually and collectively.

—The Reconstruction of the Church

Today we are reducing conversion to conversation, decision into dialogue.

—Song of Ascents

This new life will bring its own witness.

—Song of Ascents

I challenge anyone, anywhere, to expose his inner life to Jesus Christ in repentance and faith and obedience, and I will tell him what will happen—tell him with almost mathematical precision. Such a person will be changed, profoundly changed, in character and life; and he will know it in every fiber of his being

—*Song of Ascents*

Christ will take you as you are and begin to make you what you ought to be.

—*Victory Through Surrender*

If you have been a clever rascal, you can become a clever Christian—your cleverness converted and Christianized.

—*Growing Spiritually*

Conversion from wrong attitudes is just as necessary as conversion from wrong acts—perhaps more so.

—*The Way*

If we have had a bad heredity physically and spiritually, He provides us with a new heredity straight from above. There is engrafted on us a divine nature, a new heredity that cancels or controls the lower heredity—we are born from above.

—*Growing Spiritually*

The head of a medical college said to me: "If you ministers can't produce conversion we doctors will have to. For our offices are filled with people passing on the sickness of their minds and souls to their bodies and they will never be well until they change their attitudes toward life."

—*The Reconstruction of the Church*

Since conversion is a possibility, I shall be its chief illustration.

—*In Christ*

Jesus came not to get men into heaven but to get heaven into men; not to get men out of hell, but to get hell out of men.

—*The Christ of the Mount*

Will the modern age listen to the appeal for conversion? It will if those who proclaim it have it. And it will flock to the churches that illustrate it as a converted society.

—*The Reconstruction of the Church*

Something beyond forgiveness has happened—a new creation has taken place. The man who undergoes this new creation is as different from the ordinary man as the ordinary man is different from the animal.

—*Growing Spiritually*

Jesus saw the supreme danger, that men would take what He was saying as the imposition of a new code, instead of the offer of a new character.

—*The Christ of the Mount*

This possibility of conversion, regeneration, opens a new and astonishing possibility to men—that men need not remain as we are. . . . A person who doesn't take that is a fool, and I could add, a d— fool, and I wouldn't be swearing when I said it.

—*Song of Ascents*

It would be better I had not been born, if I am not reborn.

—*In Christ*

Unreconciled with God you are unreconciled with yourself, with your brother, with nature.

—*The Way*

At forty everybody should undergo reconversion on general principles. That is the period of sag.

—*The Way*

This investment in changed human character is the one bank that will not break, and it brings large dividends; it is big business.

—*Song of Ascents*

Proselytism is the coming over from one group to another group without any necessary change of character or life. It is a change of label and not of life. He saw it was a corporate egoism which wanted to add to collective power and prestige by numbers. It was essentially an irreligious process. But Jesus insisted on conversion.

—*The Reconstruction of the Church*

Conversion is that change, gradual or sudden, by which we pass from the kingdom of self at the center to the Kingdom of God at the center through the grace and power of Christ.

—*The Way*

An African, after he was converted, changed his name, calling himself, "After." Everything happened "After" he met Christ.

—*Song of Ascents*

We are always telling people that they must DO, lest they be hypocritical, while Jesus was always insisting that people BE, lest they be unreal. We are anxious about the kind of DEED; Jesus was anxious about the kind of PERSON.

—*The Christ of the Mount*

If a church is no longer able to produce, by the grace of God, the miracle of conversion, it has lost its right to be called Christian.

—*Song of Ascents*

I'm not interested in an individual gospel or a social gospel. I'm interested in one gospel that lays its hand on the individual will and says, "Repent, surrender, and be converted," and lays its hand on the collective will and says, "Repent, surrender, and be converted."

—*The Reconstruction of the Church*

Conversion is to Jesus Christ as a person and to the Kingdom of God as an order. That means that conversion is personal, a personal relationship to a Person. It also means that conversion is social, a relationship to an all-inclusive social order—the Kingdom of God.

—*Song of Ascents*

We met Christ—this living Christ, right in the midst of the roaring traffic. When I got out at the place where I was to speak, he grabbed my hand in both of his and said with deep emotion: "Thank you, I'm in." In the unshakable Kingdom—by conversion!

—*The Reconstruction of the Church*

Ninety-five percent who come to these Ashrams go away transformed.

—*Song of Ascents*

Conviction of Sin

The Gospel is disturbance before deliverance.

—*The Way*

Jesus upsets us to set us right.

—*The Way*

Creation

The touch of Christ is upon all creation.

—*The Reconstruction of the Church*

Nature works with me when I work with God, against me when I am against God.

—*The Way*

The stomach is made for goodwill, not ill will. In other words, you have a Christian stomach! Every organ in your body, every cell in your tissues, every part of your relationship with others works well in a Christian way and badly, or not at all, in an unchristian way . . . you are structured for Christ.

—*The Reconstruction of the Church*

Scratch life anywhere, and you will find a witness to the Way.

—*The Way*

The same laws are in the cell and in the farthermost star and everything between. It is a universe and not a multiverse.

—*Song of Ascents*

All lesser truths are finger posts pointing to Him who is the Truth.

—*The Way*

Jesus is the Key to the meaning of the universe. Follow the clues He gives and you get answers every time.

—*The Way*

The cross is in our blood. The white corpuscles circulate through the blood stream watching for infection. When they find it, they absorb it if possible; but when they cannot, they fling themselves upon the intruder and die that the rest may live.

—*The Way*

The judgments of life and the judgments of Christ are the same. That will be the area of the great discoveries in religion in the future.

—*The Way*

Everyone, everywhere by his makeup is destined to belong to Christ, for he is made by Christ and for Christ. Christ is his Home.

—*Song of Ascents*

God's footprints are in my tissues, in my nerves, in me.

—*The Way*

There is something in Christ that is native to my blood. He is the author of my blood. He is at home there. It flows better, is warmer and purer when He is in it. He is native to my nerves. When He controls them, they are calm and creative and contributive. He is native to every organ of my body. When He controls them they function well . . . for they are made for His control. When they get under the control of resentments, of fear, of selfishness, they function badly.

—*The Way*

Christ is in the texts of Scripture, but also in the texture of the world. He is the revelation of God and life (Rev. 3:14).

—*The Way*

There isn't a realm anywhere where the unchristian thing isn't the foolish and impossible thing.

—*The Way*

It is a universe where we get results or consequences.

—*Song of Ascents*

The difference between man and animal is not physical, but mental and spiritual.

—*The Way*

A Hindu sadhu said to me, "Please teach me how to get rid of my body—it's my enemy." That is foreign to the Christian faith. The Lord is for the body, and when the body works in His way, it works well.

—*Song of Ascents*

Man has thought he could make himself and his desires the center of the universe, thought he could become God and be happy. It has turned out badly.

—*The Way*

The earth has a destiny—the Kingdom of God is to come on it.

—*The Reconstruction of the Church*

What Jesus commands our inmost nature commends.

—*Song of Ascents*

This universe could not have happened by chance. The idea that atoms floating in space could chance upon universal law and order is absurd. How long do you think it would take for you to stand in a printing office and throw up a font of type and have it come down by chance into a poem of Longfellow?

—*Song of Ascents*

Everything has the touch of Christ upon it (Col. 1:15-16).

—*Song of Ascents*

Criticism

Don't confess the other person's sins; confess your own.

—*The Way*

Live and preach redemption, and leave judgment to God.

—*The Way*

When religious people begin backsliding, they begin back-biting.

—*The Christ of the Mount*

My tongue can have in it poison or power, but it cannot have both.

—*Growing Spiritually*

If some people were as good in telling what is wrong with them-selves as they are in telling what is wrong with others, they would be wonderful Christians. Now they are only wonderful Pharisees.

—*Growing Spiritually*

Kill the criticism before it kills the kindness.

—*Growing Spiritually*

Cynics: They have three sneers for everything and three cheers for nothing.

—*Song of Ascents*

Men are not converted by criticism. They are converted by a cross.

—*The Way*

A man criticized Moody's method of conducting a revival but did nothing himself. Moody's reply was quiet and simple. "I like my way of doing things better than your way of not doing things." The only valid criticism is the criticism of doing a better deed.

—*The Way*

The center of the Christian faith is not a judgment seat but a cross—a cross where men are not criticized but died for.

—*The Way*

If we are in the prosecution stand we are not in the witness box. If we are talking about the badness of others, we are not talking about the beauty of Jesus.

—*Growing Spiritually*

A Chinese interpreter in Malaya interrupted me when I used the word "Pharisee" with this question, "What sea is that?" I might have answered, "The Dead Sea."

—*The Way*

The way of criticism of others . . . is the way of Pharisaism. It ends in self-righteousness instead of self-realization.

—*The Way*

When you denounce, you do not announce.

—*Growing Spiritually*

When we say, "How bad he is!" we really mean, "How good I am!" This attitude of censoriousness is always the sign of a declining spiritual life.

—*The Christ of the Mount*

Sow criticism and you will reap criticism, sow love and you will reap love.

—*The Christ of the Mount*

When criticism comes, I ask, Is it true? If it is true, I will change. I am only a Christian in the making, and I'll let the criticism make me. Therefore I owe much to my critics; they are the "unpaid watchmen of my soul." Bless them!

—*The Way*

A minister was attacking me. I saw him the next day and asked how many were converted to Christ by his exposure of my many faults. I told him that I had 25 people converted at the very time he was exposing me—what was his count? "I'm out to fight the devil," he replied, unconscious that the devil was invading him, his clouded, tense face being witness.

—Growing Spiritually

I do not think the Pharisee believed for a moment that he was a hypocrite. He had said to himself so often that he thanked God he was not as other men that he came to believe it. That was the deadliness of it, for he was now sincere in his hypocrisy!

—The Christ of the Mount

The way to escape criticism is to say nothing, think nothing, and be nothing.

—Growing Spiritually

The very good Pharisee is an ugly character. Jesus made the very good Pharisee forever unrespectable.

—Growing Spiritually

Cross

When man sinned God began to suffer.

—In Christ

Jesus accomplished more in the few hours on the cross than He did in all the rest of His lifetime.

—In Christ

Our God is involved, and His involvement is a cross.

—Song of Ascents

Jesus went from equality with the Father to equality with a thief—from the highest to the lowest.

—In Christ

In the cross we see what God is like and what we must be like.

—Song of Ascents

Only at the cross can you see your sins.

—In Christ

The cross is the price God pays to get to us in spite of our sins.

—The Way

I grow up only as I go up—to Calvary. I die to live.

—The Way

God cannot save without a cross. The cross is the price God must pay to get to us in spite of our sin. Self-giving on the part of God and man is the crux of the Christian faith.

—*In Christ*

Jesus aligned Himself with self-giving instead of self-saving. In doing so He revealed the deepest thing in the heart of God—self-sacrifice, the Lamb at the heart of the throne. . . . He rules from a cross.

—*Victory Through Surrender*

God wrapped His heart in flesh and blood and let it break upon a cross.

—*Growing Spiritually*

If a spotlight from Mars were to be pointed at the most important place on our planet, it would fall upon a hill called Calvary.

—*The Way*

The Man who never used the word "hope" has put Hope into the lives of millions of hopeless beings. The Man who "descended into hell" has lifted more people out of the hell of meaningless and disrupted living than all the philosophers and moralists combined.

—*Growing Spiritually*

Many try to obtain peace by their own blood, their own struggles and sacrifice; but it's not by our blood, but His!

—*Growing Spiritually*

The historical must become the experiential or it isn't redemption.

—*In Christ*

The cross shall be not merely on my church, it shall be in my consciousness—my working way to live.

—*In Christ*

Christianity is pessimism turned into optimism—the cross turned into an Easter morning.

—*Growing Spiritually*

When the cross becomes a mere symbol on churches, or becomes a hard doctrine, or becomes a cheap easy way of salvation which costs us nothing but faith, leaving the essential self untouched, and not demanding that we face life in the same spirit of self-sacrificial giving, then it has turned to darkness.

—*The Christ of the Mount*

They asserted themselves; he surrendered Himself.

—*In Christ*

This forgiveness based upon the goodness and love of God, but without the atoning sacrifice of Himself, is a forgiveness that is shallow, without moral content, and will not and does not produce human self-giving.

—*Song of Ascents*

The Cross was sin, and He turned it into redemption from sin; the Cross was hate, and He turned it into a revelation of love; the Cross was man at his worst, and Jesus through it showed God at His redemptive best.

—*Growing Spiritually*

Two great powers joined in crucifying Jesus—the power of religion, represented by the high priests, and the power of the state, represented by Pilate and his Roman officers and soldiers. He disarmed them both, made a public showing of them.

—*In Christ*

Culture

THE HERD/THE UNBELIEVING WORLD

The reason for the passionate demand for entertainment and diversion is that the well within is dry.

—*The Way*

Whatever gets your attention gets you.

—*Victory Through Surrender*

You are no longer herd-centered when you are surrendered to God. "Everybody does it" is replaced by, "This is what He would have me do." You are delivered from herd-domination.

—*Victory Through Surrender*

The dominance of the herd over the individual is responsible for more collapsed moral standards, lowered tones of spiritual life, than any other single thing.

—*The Way*

If you stand for nothing, you will fall for anything.

—*The Way*

Paul made the grain of everyday happenings into the bread of the Kingdom.

—*In Christ*

The Christian faith says that you must lose your life in a higher purpose and a higher will and then you will find it. The secular city mentality and outlook says the opposite—find yourself by asserting and looking after yourself in every possible way, in every situation possible.

—*The Reconstruction of the Church*

The life of the modern man seems so full. He is preoccupied with many things, but down underneath these outer things there is a growing emptiness.

—*In Christ*

Ours is a cut-flower civilization. We are living without roots. Our morality has no roots in the cosmic order, but only in changing customs and they fade. Our happiness has no cosmic backing and hence it too easily withers and dies.

—*The Way*

Society demands conformity. If you fall beneath its standards it will punish you; if you rise above its standards it will persecute you.

—*The Way*

Jesus is Lord of all or not Lord at all.

—*Growing Spiritually*

If the Church is wedded to the spirit of the day it will be a widow tomorrow.

—*Victory Through Surrender*

Surrender to the herd instinct is the most dangerous thing in life. Jesus was crucified by it.

—*The Way*

Some people succumb to noise to give themselves release from themselves.

—*Growing Spiritually*

I master the world around me, provided Jesus Christ masters the world within me.

—*In Christ*

The vogue turns to the vague and the vague to the vacuum and the vacuum compels one to turn to listen to Christ the Real, the Realizer, the Redeemer.

—*The Reconstruction of the Church*

We are in the process of being standardized morally—at a very low level.

—*The Way*

In the view of secularism the Kingdom of God is not the doing of the will of God on earth as it is done in heaven; it is the acceptance of the secular city as the Kingdom.

—*The Reconstruction of the Church*

Now the demand is. . .to accept this secular order as the Kingdom of God. The "Secular City" is the Kingdom. In other words, the flesh has become the Word.

—*The Reconstruction of the Church*

People say that we must adopt the language and culture of the day to be relevant to today. That is a mistake. If the church marries itself to the spirit of the times, it will be a widow in the next generation.

—*Song of Ascents*

To ape an age to get that age is futile.

—*The Reconstruction of the Church*

He who disregards the past will find the future disregarding him.

—*The Christ of the Mount*

This division between the secular and the sacred persists today—a disastrous division. It destroys the essential nature of Christianity.

—*In Christ*

The division of life between the material and the spiritual is a false division. In the Christian faith they are one. Unless the spiritual functions in material terms it doesn't function.

—*The Reconstruction of the Church*

We become like that which we worship.

—*Growing Spiritually*

Death

He cleansed the grave from decay and made it Resurrection.

—*In Christ*

Death has no sting for the Christian; its sting has been pulled at the Cross.

—*Growing Spiritually*

All life separated from Christ is in process of decay.

—*In Christ*

Many people are so closely linked with their bodies that the decay of the body means the decay of the person.

—*Growing Spiritually*

Some have had an adequate chance in this life to be in Christ and have decided against it. They decide to be in themselves. They have chosen death, and if they take death out with them they will have death forever.

—*In Christ*

Democracy

This is the basis of democracy: equal before God and therefore equal before men.

—*In Christ*

The only faith that can sustain a democracy is the Christian faith, and that faith interpreted by evangelical Christianity.

—*In Christ*

The fact is that the Christian faith is father or grandfather of almost everything fine in Western civilization. Take Christianity out as the root and the fruit will wither.

—*Song of Ascents*

India struggling to be a democracy, which is corporate caring, has difficulty in producing that corporate caring. For at the center of her philosophy is a noncaring god—Brahman, the impersonal Nirguna, the unrelated. . . . They need the conception of the serving God to produce serving men.

—*Song of Ascents*

DISCIPLINE

There is no use trying to discipline yourself until you surrender yourself.

—*Song of Ascents*

Only as I am disciplined can I dance the dance of freedom.

—*The Way*

Be disciplined or be decadent.

—*The Way*

Civilizations have organized themselves around rivers, not swamps. Some people are rivers: they know where they want to go and they confine themselves to the banks that lead to the goal. But some people are swamps: they spread over everything; their minds are so open they cannot hold a conviction; they are everything and nothing.

—*Song of Ascents*

You cannot have an undisciplined life and be beautiful.

—*The Way*

People who try to be free through indiscipline are "free" in the sense that a ship is free when it has lost both compass and rudder.

—*Growing Spiritually*

Sex is the best servant we can have—and the worst master.

—*Growing Spiritually*

He did not guard his inner life, so his outer life came down in ruin around him. Discipline the inner self by a complete self-surrender to God.

—*The Way*

If perfection and not pleasure be the goal, then this universe had to be a universe of discipline, of pain, and even of hardness. I need this kind of school if my graduation means that.

—*The Christ of the Mount*

Discipline the beginnings. The ends are in the beginnings.

—*The Way*

If you are not faithful in a trifle, you cannot be trusted with the tremendous. If you are not faithful with the material, how can you be entrusted with the spiritual—the "true Riches?"

—*Growing Spiritually*

He cared little for his character and everything for his reputation. He tried to discipline a reputation, leaving his undisciplined character untouched.

—*The Way*

If anyone could find God through disciplined effort, Mahatma Gandhi should have found Him.

—*Song of Ascents*

A brother prayed very often, "Fill me, Lord." A man nearby was overheard to say, "You can't, Lord. He leaks!" God isn't going to pour the water of His grace down the rat-holes of undisciplined living.

—*The Way*

Double-mindedness

No heart is big enough for two mutually exclusive loves.

—*The Way*

You can serve God with Mammon, but you cannot serve God and Mammon.

—*The Way*

I am a Christian—I lean on no staff that will break and pierce my hand and heart.

—*The Way*

A sign over an express office in Shanghai said: "Your baggage taken and delivered in all directions." We must decide to be one person, with one motive toward one goal.

—*The Way*

A Hindu said one day in a public meeting: "Stanley Jones is so broad and liberal." I replied: "My brother, I am perhaps the narrowest man you have ever seen. I am a man of one book, one Person, one message, and one intention—to give that message."

—*Song of Ascents*

"My name is Legion"—that was the basis of his torment. He was not one person, he was many persons, and many contradictory persons, "a walking civil war." And yet he was religious.

—*Victory Through Surrender*

The purification of loyalties is the essence of purification. If there is anything in your life about which you cannot pray, bring it up relentlessly and expose it to God's presence and to His suggestions.

—*The Way*

EDUCATION

My religious education will educate me beyond religion to a saving relationship to Jesus.

—*In Christ*

Religious education can become salvation by process instead of salvation by a Person.

—*In Christ*

You've grasped the principles, but you've missed the Person.

—*Song of Ascents*

Intelligence not linked with goodness is no longer intelligence—it is learned ignorance.

—*The Way*

The more I know of Jesus the more I know of God.

—*Song of Ascents*

To know Him more clearly; to love Him more dearly; to obey Him more nearly—these sum up the total growth of the total person.

—*Growing Spiritually*

In His being primarily "Teacher" you are religious; in His being primarily "Lord" you are His, you are a Christian.

—*Victory Through Surrender*

Jesus said: "Come . . . Take . . . Learn." . . . Religious education, for the most part, with some exceptions, reverses the process and says, "Learn . . . Take . . . Come." Often the process doesn't get as far as "take,"or "come"; it stops at the "learn." Insofar as it does, it ends in sterile knowledge.

—*Growing Spiritually*

Wisdom that has an unsurrendered egocentricity at its heart is foolishness—the foolishness, for instance, on the part of psychiatry that knowledge, or insight, will cure you of mental or emotional sicknesses. It doesn't.

—*In Christ*

To be taught about Him is verbal theology; to be taught in Him is vital Christianity.

—*In Christ*

Our churches are filled with people who have come up through religious education who lack the consciousness of Life. They have not been spiritually recreated, nor can they spiritually re-create.

—*In Christ*

Somewhere along the way the knowledge about Jesus must turn to a knowledge of Jesus—a knowledge of Him as personal Savior and Lord. This comes through repentance, through surrender, through receiving Christ into the heart and enthroning Him there as Lord by faith.

—*In Christ*

Jesus is knowledge turned wise. . . . It is not merely religious wisdom; it is all wisdom.

—*In Christ*

The wisest person in the world is the person who acts upon the principles and mind of Jesus.

—*In Christ*

Enemies

This is a simple way to get rid of enemies. Have no enmity and your enemies are all gone, at least so far as you are concerned.

—*The Way*

Eternal Life / Heaven

We will start in heaven with the capacity for the enjoyment of God we have developed here.

—*Growing Spiritually*

Everyone's cup will be full, but some cups will be larger.

—*Growing Spiritually*

If immortality goes, then immorality comes.

—*Growing Spiritually*

In Jesus there are no sunsets; they are all sunrises.

—*Song of Ascents*

I belong to the future, for I belong to Jesus Christ, and the future belongs to Him.

—*Song of Ascents*

I cannot live on the promise of a home—I must live in a home. I cannot live on a heaven hereafter, I must live in a heaven now.

—*In Christ*

EVANGELISM

Nothing is really mine until I share it.

—*The Way*

We should be ringing door bells instead of church bells.

—*The Way*

If you are not winning others, Christ has not really won you.

—*In Christ*

There are many who are afraid to speak to others about Christ, for they are afraid of making mistakes. But the biggest mistake is not to do it. If a man doesn't make mistakes, he doesn't make anything else.

—*Growing Spiritually*

No life is Christian that is not Christianizing.

—*The Christ of the Mount*

The redeemed become the redeeming.

—*In Christ*

Philip was at home in two worlds at once. He served tables as a deacon, but he won people to Christ as an evangelist, and the two were not two, but one.

—*The Way*

To know Him and to help others to know Him.

—*Growing Spiritually*

I am called to be an evangelist and missionary, and I hereby resign as a bishop-elect of the Methodist Church.

—*Song of Ascents*

Taking and telling, the alternate beats of the Christian heart. When something happens to us, then something happens through us.

—*The Way*

If we are not reconciling, we are not Christian.

—*The Way*

I will not remain evangelical unless I become evangelistic.

—*The Way*

The Bride is the church. Those who belong to the Bride, the invisible church, say, "Come." And if they do not say, "Come," they do not belong to the invisible church, even though they may belong to the visible church.

—*The Reconstruction of the Church*

"Christian": it wasn't a name plastered on them, it was a name projected from them!

—*The Reconstruction of the Church*

When I arrive in heaven I will ask for twenty-four hours of rest. Then I will ask for twenty-four hours to visit with my friends and renew old acquaintances. Then I would like to go up to Jesus and say, "This is wonderful, and I do not deserve to be here; grace has brought me home and I love it here. But haven't you a world that is fallen, and needs an evangelist? Please send me." . . . I know of no heaven more heavenly than proclaiming the good news of Jesus Christ.

—*Song of Ascents*

Nothing really lives that isn't life-giving.

—*The Way*

The Christian is not in the business of winning arguments, but of winning people.

—*Song of Ascents*

An English bishop said, "Wherever Paul went he started a revolution. Wherever I go they serve me tea."

—*Song of Ascents*

A set of beliefs to be believed, or a moralism to be followed, both leave the essential self untouched.

—*Victory Through Surrender*

The apostles gave up this work of serving tables so they could be evangelistic. But, strangely enough, the only man who had the title "evangelist" was the man who had a layman's job thrust upon him and was not supposed to do evangelistic work. But the impulse was greater than the imposition. The reach of his soul went beyond the reach of his hand; he shared a gospel as well as goods.

—*The Way*

If dialogue ends in dialogue and stops this side of the objective decision, it is verbal and not vital, and less than Christian.

—*Song of Ascents*

If he receives the Gospel and doesn't give the Gospel what one has turns out to be less than the Gospel and other than the Gospel.

—*The Reconstruction of the Church*

I gave an altar call at each night service, and for four years every Sunday we had conversions, except for two Sundays; and on those two Sundays it was too hot for anybody to decide anything. In Lucknow there are two seasons—six months of Paradise and six months of Purgatory.

—*Song of Ascents*

Our greatest need is laymen on fire with evangelism.

—The Way

As soon as one finds Christ there is an impulse to find another and bring him to Christ.

—The Way

To be an evangelist and a Christian is difficult. To be any professionally religious person and a Christian is difficult.

—Song of Ascents

This verse is my verse, given to me when I began my work as a missionary and evangelist. I have lived on that verse all these years. John 15:16—"You have not chosen Me, but I have chosen you, and ordained you, that you should go and bring forth fruit, and that your fruit should remain: that whatsoever you shall ask of the Father in my name, he may give it you."

If there is no impulse to share it, then the life within is dead or moribund. For the creative impulse is within this new life by its very nature. Evangelism, therefore, is not something imposed. It is inherent.

—The Way

The difference between contending for the faith and commending the faith by lifting up Christ is the difference between unchristianity and Christianity. One is egocentric and the other is Christ-centric . . . One tries to win an argument and the other tries to win the man.

—In Christ

The end of evangelism is to produce an evangelist.

—The Way

Two things characterize the real Christian: he listens to God, and he talks to people.

—The Way

New converts make the best evangelists.

—In Christ

If you do not give you haven't got.

—The Reconstruction of the Church

Jesus is on trial again before the world, and every one of His disciples is called in as a defense witness. Suppose we refuse to say a word on His behalf; then by our silence we join the prosecution. For He said, "He that is not with me is against me."

—Growing Spiritually

The question at the end of a Sunday service should be, not "how many people gathered?" but "how many were sent out from that gathering to shake the world?"

—*The Reconstruction of the Church*

You are a Christian, and you can be a Christian only as you try to Christianize others.

—*Growing Spiritually*

I have never taken a penny for preaching the gospel. For forty-three years, since I began writing books, I have turned everything I've earned through my evangelistic meetings and other speaking engagements into my work in India; taking part of the earnings of my books for my living expenses and giving the rest for the work in India and elsewhere.

—*Song of Ascents*

A Christian that is not witnessing will soon have nothing to witness to.

—*The Reconstruction of the Church*

We must now cease to embalm it. We must embody it—or abdicate.

—*The Christ of the Mount*

If we do not evangelize we will evaporate. It will be the twilight of the Christian movement.

—*The Reconstruction of the Church*

Many are so afraid of making a mistake that they don't make anything else! They have so much tact that they have no contact.

—*Growing Spiritually*

Religion that treats outer symptoms and leaves untouched the central disease, the unsurrendered self, is religious quackery.

—*Victory Through Surrender*

A man was talking about the glory of the church of Westminster Abbey. A little woman spoke up and said, "Has anyone been saved here lately?" It was a good question . . . for no heart is pure that is not passionate, no virtue is safe that is not enthusiastic, and no life is Christian that is not Christianizing.

—*Growing Spiritually*

God's highest and most climactic word: Evangelism!

—*The Reconstruction of the Church*

FAITH

Faith is a surrender to the will of God. . . . You cannot have faith unless you are committed to God.

—The Way

I am not trusting my faith, but my faith is trusting Thee!

—The Way

If our faith costs nothing, it contributes nothing.

—The Way

If Jesus is the center of our faith He will be the center of our affections.

—The Reconstruction of the Church

Christ, and not merely doctrines about Him, is the fundamental center of your faith.

—The Way

We are not saved by faith, but by faith in Christ.

—The Way

FEAR / WORRY

Worry is like a rocking chair—it will give you something to do but won't get you anywhere.

—Growing Spiritually

Worry is an old man with bended head, carrying a load of feathers which he thinks are lead.

—The Way

A pastor suggests an added collection in which we pass the collection plate and drop into it our fears and anxieties. Then take them to the foot of the cross and bury them.

—Growing Spiritually

Forethought is essentially God-centered; anxiety is essentially self-centered.

—In Christ

If you conceal a fear, it will be driven into the subconscious, and there it will work havoc. Bring it up and out and look at it.

—Growing Spiritually

You can see the stars even in the daytime from the bottom of a well.

—The Way

FORGIVENESS

The most blessed fact of the Christian gospel is the offer of divine forgiveness.

—Growing Spiritually

God cannot forgive the unforgiving.

—*Growing Spiritually*

Do not spend useless time worrying about a past you cannot change. He forgives; let that suffice.

—*The Way*

There are no skeletons in the Christian's closet, for they have all come out and are clothed in flesh and blood and walk as witnesses of the saving power of Christ.

—*Growing Spiritually*

When a Roman persecutor said to a Christian who was in the tyrant's grip, "What can your Master do for you now?" the man replied, "He can help me to forgive you." That forgiveness was the victory!

—*In Christ*

Freedom

Bound to Him, I walk the earth free.

—*In Christ*

We are free to choose, but we are not free to choose the results of our choosing.

—*The Way*

Any supposed freedom that leaves you with an impure heart, a bad conscience, and an insincere faith ends not in springing and singing, but in sighing and dying.

—*The Way*

Liberty comes through obedience to law.

—*The Way*

Bound to Him you walk the earth free! Low at His feet you stand straight before everything else!

—*Victory Through Surrender*

There is a false idea of freedom prevalent in modern civilization: "You are free to do as you like." The Christian answer is, "You are free to do as you ought."

—*The Way*

The most deadly of mistakes is the mistake of thinking that our way against God's way can ever lead us to freedom.

—*Growing Spiritually*

The ideas underlying the Sermon on the Mount are the charter of freedom to all men, of all races, of all climes, of all classes.

—*The Christ of the Mount*

There is no freedom without discipline.

—*Song of Ascents*

Paul, in Nero's prison, was not Nero's prisoner.

—*In Christ*

Bondage to prestige is bondage.

—*The Way*

GIVING

As I take from Infinity, I can give infinitely.

—*In Christ*

Half-giving results in half-living.

—*Growing Spiritually*

I ask not for tasks equal to my powers, but for powers equal to my tasks, and may they be big ones!

—*Growing Spiritually*

There is only one place where you can invest life and money and not lose it—in people.

—*The Christ of the Mount*

If the outer without the inner is hypocrisy, so the inner without the outer is also hypocrisy.

—*The Reconstruction of the Church*

GOSPEL

The gospel is not a demand, it is an offer.

—*Song of Ascents*

The gospel is not the echo of Sinai, but the voice of Calvary.

—*The Christ of the Mount*

The gospel begins with Jesus, not with God. Apart from Jesus you know little or nothing about God and what you know is wrong.

—*Song of Ascents*

There are many religions, but one gospel.

—*Song of Ascents*

Quacks treat symptoms, doctors treat diseases.

—*Victory Through Surrender*

Everything they brought up was the Word become word, and what the gospel presented was the Word become flesh.

—*Song of Ascents*

Can we expect the gospel to do everything for us unless we take everything it has?

—*The Christ of the Mount*

Grace Offered and Received

We are saved by God's grace, not by our good works.

—*In Christ*

Empty your hands and take the Gift of God.

—*Song of Ascents*

Admiral Sato, commander of the Japanese fleet of submarines at Pearl Harbor: "If I can't get in because I'm good, maybe I can get in because I'm evil." And he did.

—*Song of Ascents*

You must choose between the grace of Life or the law of life. One produces the Christian, the other produces the Pharisee. One surrenders and trusts, the other struggles and struts. One lives by an obtainment and the other lives by an attainment. The one is an artesian well, the other is force pump. One says, "Love God and do what you like." The other grimly says, "I must do what I don't like."

—*The Way*

If you take the gift, you belong forever to the Giver.

—*Song of Ascents*

Instead of us meeting (God) on the topmost rung of the ladder of worthiness, He comes down and meets us at the bottommost rung as sinners.

—*Song of Ascents*

Be poor enough to receive and the Kingdom of heaven is yours; all its resources and power are yours (Matt. 5:3).

—*Song of Ascents*

No one is farther from God than one word—Yes.

—*Song of Ascents*

A lack of consent and cooperation ties God's hands.

—*The Way*

Grace sought me, Grace bought me, Grace taught me, Grace caught me—now Grace has me.

—*The Way*

A leper said to me, "Everybody said to me, 'Go,' but only Jesus said to me, 'Come!' "

—*The Reconstruction of the Church*

Grace is free, but when you take it you are bound forever to the Giver.

—*The Way*

Ask . . . accept . . . give . . . obey.

—*The Way*

Mahatma Gandhi was trying to find God through attainment, a disciplined attainment. I found God through obtainment—through grace. One is self-salvation; the other is God-salvation.

—*Song of Ascents*

Jesus was the revealer of the nature of reality, and in that Reality the most beautiful thing revealed is Grace.

—*The Way*

You don't grow into grace; you grow when you are IN it.

—*Growing Spiritually*

Grace makes you gracious, the Giver makes you give.

—*The Way*

"Take what you want," says God, "and pay for it." And the paying? It is not our goodness, but our gratitude. Not our worthiness, but our willingness.

—*The Way*

Always get a task you can't do, one that is beyond your powers. That throws you back on divine grace.

—*The Way*

This shift from legalism to redemptive grace is one of the most deeply needed shifts in a reconstructed church.

—*The Reconstruction of the Church*

Prayer: O Thou eternal Christ, understandable even to me, I thank You for putting the latch-string so low I can reach it. I can reach the Highest, for You are the Highest become lowly, reachable. And so I come, for in You I see everything I need. I thank you. Amen.

—*The Way*

Growing Spiritually

Someone has defined adolescence as "a period of temporary insanity."

—*The Way*

No good shall keep me from the better, no better keep me from the best.

—*Growing Spiritually*

What you want determines what you will be. "Desire is king."

—*The Christ of the Mount*

I have learned the bitter lesson of how not to live. I am learning the better lesson of how to live.

—*The Way*

Every soul is stunted until it puts its taproot down into God and begins to draw sustenance from the Divine. If it lives upon the surface roots of a mere intellectual and material life, it will remain stunted and dwarfed.

—*The Christ of the Mount*

Impression minus expression equals depression.

—*Song of Ascents*

Anything that leaves you at the center is off-center.

—*Victory Through Surrender*

Just as the mariner on the sea has to get his bearings from the stars to be able to put into the right earthly port, so we have to get our eternal values straight before we can get our temporal values straight.

—*The Way*

The stages through which we pass to maturity: dependence (childhood); independence (adolescence); interdependence (maturity).

—*The Way*

The only thing you believe in is the thing you believe in enough to practice. Your creed is your deed.

—*The Reconstruction of the Church*

Don't struggle to grow; surrender to grow. Empty your hands and take the gift.

—*Growing Spiritually*

A man stood up in a meeting and said: "Twenty years ago my cup was filled, and since that nary a drop has gone into it and nary a drop has come out of it." Another, hearing, said: "Then by this time there must be wiggle-tails in it!"

—*Growing Spiritually*

I would treat others as Christ treats me.

—*Song of Ascents*

An arid liberalism and an acrid conservatism are both alike sterile. Together they could be fruitful.

—*The Way*

The ladder to abundant life: (1) Consider your ways; (2) Change your directions; (3) Connect with Christ; (4) Consent to surrender; (5) Cease from struggling; (6) Concentrate on acceptance; (7) Cleanse your past (forgiveness and restitution); (8) Christianize your relationships; (9) Cultivate the Quiet Time; (10) Create outlets and activities (helping others).

—*The Way*

We need a radical conservatism and a conservative radicalism. Jesus was both.

—*The Way*

First faith, then fact, and then feeling.

—*Victory Through Surrender*

A real radical has the root of the past in him, but demands that that root bear fruit now in the total life. He demands that implications become applications.

—*The Way*

The past married to the future brings forth the living present. But conservatism married to nothing but itself, or radicalism married to nothing but itself, brings forth nothing—nothing but controversy or conjecture.

—*The Way*

I shall be a conservative in my faith and a radical in its application.

—*The Way*

It is practical if you practice it.

—*Song of Ascents*

Some have just enough religion to produce irritation and not enough to produce iridescence.

—*The Way*

In Christ I see the incredible, know the unknowable, and do the impossible.

—*Growing Spiritually*

Make a framework of habits in which God is first, others second, and you third.

—*Growing Spiritually*

Words and deeds are the two wings of the Christian as he soars and sings.

—*The Reconstruction of the Church*

You have been doing everything for the love of self; now do everything for the love of God.

—*Growing Spiritually*

My aim in life: all my actions and all my reactions Christian!

—*Growing Spiritually*

A rut is defined as a grave with both ends knocked out.

—*The Reconstruction of the Church*

It is a working principle or it is a worthless principle.

—*The Reconstruction of the Church*

Sow a thought and you reap an act; sow an act and you reap a habit; sow a habit and you reap a character; sow a character and you reap a destiny.

—*The Christ of the Mount*

If I were to pick out two phrases necessary for spiritual growth, I would pick these: "I don't know" and "I am sorry."

—Song of Ascents

If you won't live with Christ, you can't live with yourself.

—The Reconstruction of the Church

There is a once-for-all surrender, and there is a continuous, day-by-day surrender.

—Victory Through Surrender

You do not gain Christ through self-control; you gain self-control through Christ.

—Growing Spiritually

Self-surrender is the most emancipating, the most universalizing thing imaginable.

—Victory Through Surrender

I could accept and work with people and love them even if I saw imperfections in them. Knowing that Jesus accepted me with all my imperfections made it easier to accept others with all their imperfections.

—Song of Ascents

A man's size is determined by the size of the things that upset him.

—Sat Tal Ashram wall mottoes

"I am the tadpole of an archangel," someone cried. But I am more: I am the embryo of the man who is to be perfect as the Father is perfect. Then let nothing stop me. . . . O littleness lay no cramping hand on me, for I am made for the great; O flesh, do not ensnare me, for I am out for high destiny; O world, teach me, but do not entangle me, for the perfect calls me. And I must go.

—The Christ of the Mount

Your ability to look at yourself objectively without attempting to defend yourself, or excuse yourself, will be the measure of your growth and maturity.

—Growing Spiritually

Keep your eyes on your blessings, not on your blightings.

—Growing Spiritually

"Love Christ and do as you like, for you will like what He likes.

—Growing Spiritually

Faithfulness in the little becomes fruitfulness in the big.

—Growing Spiritually

The business of my life, and the only business of my life, is to abide in Him. All else follows.

—In Christ

They are living on the menu instead of the meat.

—In Christ

You can be rich in two ways: the abundance of your possessions or the fewness of your wants.

—The Way

Your self in your own hands is a problem and a pain; your self in God's hands is a power and a possibility.

—Victory Through Surrender

GUIDANCE

Be Christ-directed instead of circumstance directed.

—The Way

Without Thee, not one step over the threshold; with Thee, anywhere!

—The Way

Suspect any guidance that doesn't fit in with the character and life and teaching of Jesus. When in doubt, do the most Christlike thing and you won't go wrong.

—The Reconstruction of the Church

If we take our own way in the ordinary, we can't expect God to give us His way in the hour of need.

—The Way

There may be guidance in the absence of guidance; the guidance is to trust where you cannot see.

—The Way

An individual guidance that isn't subjected to a group guidance is liable to go off in tangents.

—Growing Spiritually

He cannot guide us in the occasional unless we let Him guide us in the continual.

—Growing Spiritually

If there is no Hand on my helm, there will be rocks beneath my bow.

—The Way

Don't ask for the whole way; ask for the next step.

—The Way

I felt if God guides, God provides.

—Song of Ascents

HATE

How can hate have any part of me? For I belong to a Man who died on a tree—for those who hated Him.

—The Way

Hatred consumes the consumer.

—*The Way*

Health

To be good is good for you. To be bad is bad for you.

—*The Way*

Guilt produces conflict, and conflict wears out the physical organism.

—*The Way*

I do not think that I should drink, for when I drink I do not think.

—*The Way*

The right thing morally is always the healthy thing physically . . . economically . . . sociologically . . . educationally . . . politically.

—*The Way*

A man was so addicted that he set his alarm clock at twelve every night to wake himself so he could take his sleeping tablets.

—*Growing Spiritually*

There is some conflict at the root of every nervous breakdown. The cause of the conflict must be found and adjusted.

—*The Way*

The causes of tiredness: (1) self-centeredness; (2) boredom; (3) worry; (4) fear; (5) inferiority feelings; (6) resentments; (7) indecision; (8) oversensitivity; and (9) inner guilts.

—*The Way*

The cigarette is a minus sign.

—*The Way*

L.C.C.—lung cancer candidate.

—*Song of Ascents*

You cannot hurt another without hurting yourself.

—*The Way*

It is infinite Sanctity and infinite Sanity.

—*Growing Spiritually*

The greatest medicine for health is conversion. The greatest tonic for the toning up of the whole system is the Holy Spirit, and the greatest vitamin known is love. The greatest physical therapy is creative work.

—*Song of Ascents*

Healing by the direct touch of God— I know it. For I was suddenly touched in a dark moment, and from that time I've known health and life.

—*The Way*

Paul: when his eyesight went bad his insight went better.

—*Song of Ascents*

The twelve apostles of ill health: anger, resentments, fear, worry, desire to dominate, self-preoccupation, guilts, sexual impurity, jealousy, a lack of creative activity, inferiorities, a lack of love.

—*Song of Ascents*

HOLY SPIRIT

We occupy ourselves with the marginal, and do not appropriate the central.

—*The Christ of the Mount*

Baptism with water cannot unite us, for it is not the "one baptism" which Jesus came to give—it is marginal. The baptism of the Spirit is central.

—*In Christ*

The Spirit cannot witness through me unless He witnesses to me.

—*In Christ*

In the light of the world's emptiness I have no right to be empty when God offers me the fullness of the Spirit.

—*The Way*

Purity and Power: Two things are permanent in the gift of the Holy Spirit: purity and power. Purity for myself and my own inner needs, and power to witness effectively to others.

—*Song of Ascents*

It's pouring down, it's pouring down—take it!

—*Song of Ascents*

I deserve nothing; I have everything.

—*Song of Ascents*

Some of us show childish delight in little "blessings," and all the time here is this Central Resource, the mighty overflowing, life-giving Spirit, who would turn our hearts and our society from a desert to a veritable garden of the Lord.

—*The Christ of the Mount*

Spirit-control ends in self-control. The self-control is not the control that sits on a lid but a control through surrender of the self to the Holy Spirit.

—*The Way*

We are afraid to turn on the power—it's here unused. That power is nothing less than the power of the Holy Spirit.

—*The Way*

The Indwelling is the focal point of redemption. Without Indwelling, redemption doesn't get at us where it counts.

—*The Way*

I was released from the fear of emotion. I had tasted three days of ecstasy—drunk with God. And yet they were the clearest-headed, soberest moments I have ever known. I saw into the heart of reality, and the heart of reality was joy, joy, joy. And the heart of reality was love, love, love.

—*Song of Ascents*

I dropped on my knees beside my bed, and said: "Now, Lord, what shall I do?" And He replied: "Will you give me your all?" And after a moment's hesitation I replied: "Yes, Lord, of course I will. I will give you my all, all I know and all I don't know." Then He replied: "Then take my all, take the Holy Spirit." I paused a moment: my all for His all: my all was myself, His all was Himself, the Holy Spirit. I saw in a flash the offer. I eagerly replied: "I will take the Holy Spirit." I arose from my knees, with no evidence, save His word. I walked out on the naked promise of that Word.

—*Song of Ascents*

I opened every portion of my being and let it rain all over me. He has come, and at His touch the desert began to blossom as the rose.

—*The Christ of the Mount*

When suddenly I was filled—filled with the Holy Spirit, wave after wave of the Spirit seemed to be going through me as a cleansing fire. I could only walk the floor with tears of joy flowing down my cheeks. I could do nothing but praise Him—and did. I knew this was no passing emotion; the Holy Spirit has come to abide with me forever.

—*Song of Ascents*

A woman put it this way: "Apart from the Holy spirit, Brother Stanley would be a mess." She was right. But with the Holy Spirit I am not a mess, but a message, for I have a message.

—*Song of Ascents*

We must not be half-filled vessels trying to run over.

—*In Christ*

The modes of life come out of the conscious, but the moods of life come out of the subconscious.

—*Victory Through Surrender*

The subconscious was redeemed. These drives which reside in the subconscious—self, sex, and the herd—were cleansed . . . it was conversion unlimited!

—*Song of Ascents*

How can we distinguish between the voice of the subconscious and the voice of God? The voice of the subconscious argues with you to try to convince you. The voice of God doesn't argue; it speaks, and the words are self-verifying.

—*The Reconstruction of the Church*

God FOR us, the divine Intention, the Father; God WITH us, the divine Invasion, the Son; God IN us, the divine Indwelling, the Holy Spirit. Our need is within us. There must be Indwelling.

—*The Way*

This was not a remembrance of Christ; it was a realization of Christ. Every fiber of my being sang His praise. . . . Then one day I looked into my heart to see the thornbush which I had planted there on Good Friday and lo, it was all abloom with the Rose of Sharon . . . I chose a Calvary and found an Easter morning.

—*Song of Ascents*

Turn over all you know—the conscious—and all you don't know—the subconscious—and the Holy Spirit will take over the subconscious and will cleanse and coordinate and make it peaceful and calm with His presence and His power.

—*Growing Spiritually*

You are a marked man—the mark of Christ is on you.

—*Song of Ascents*

A year after I met Christ I had been led into two vital things—the new birth and the fullness of the Holy Spirit. One brought me into the Kingdom and the other brought the Kingdom into me.

—*Song of Ascents*

Know thyself, accept thyself, develop thyself—that is pagan. Surrender thyself, discipline thyself, obey Another Self—the Spirit of God—that is Christian.

—*The Way*

I am not controlled by pleasures from within or pressures from without. I am controlled from above.

—*Growing Spiritually*

The subconscious is the place of peace or unpeace.

—*Growing Spiritually*

Not power pumped up through human organization, but power poured down into human receptivity.

—*The Reconstruction of the Church*

The Christian has the Spirit and the Spirit has the Christian.

—*The Way*

You cannot make your mind good unless you make God's mind your goodness.

—*The Christ of the Mount*

Can we have the gift of the Holy Spirit without the gift of tongues? The answer is simple: Did Jesus have the Holy Spirit? Yes. Did He speak in tongues? And the answer is No. Then I can have the Holy Spirit without the gift of tongues.

—*Song of Ascents*

The emphasis was upon the gift of the Spirit instead of the gifts of the Spirit.

—*Song of Ascents*

Where the gift of tongues is not taught or expected, it seldom or never happens.

—*Song of Ascents*

God has come a long way in His approach to me. He has come through an incarnation, an atoning death, a resurrection, down to the door of my heart. Having come so far, I know He will come the full way—He will come within me. The Holy Spirit is God coming within me.

—*The Way*

Had the disciples tried to bypass Pentecost, we would never have heard of them again. They would have exhausted themselves against the problems of that day.

—*The Way*

The Holy Spirit is not central in our present-day Christianity. The emphasis upon the Holy Spirit has been pushed from the main stream of Christianity into the cults.

—*The Way*

In the new birth you have the Holy Spirit; in the fullness the Holy Spirit has you. Before Pentecost the disciples had the Holy Spirit, but after Pentecost the Holy Spirit had them.

—*The Way*

John's baptism was with water, to get rid of; Jesus' baptism was with the Spirit, to get possession of. . . . John irritated; Jesus inspired.

—*The Way*

The queer have queered Pentecost for many. And yet the almost entire absence of emphasis on the Spirit has impoverished the main stream of Christianity. It often degenerates into a humanistic striving to be good.

—The Way

When surrendered to the Spirit we become inwardly harmonized and hence outwardly effective.

—The Way

As a child of God I am heir to the best the Father has—Himself. I take the gift of the Holy Spirit and I take Him now.

—The Way

If you have the Spirit you have love, and if you do not have love, you do not have the Spirit.

—Growing Spiritually

I know I would not be called to walk in the Way without being provided with power to walk in the Way.

—The Way

Pentecost divorced from the Sermon on the Mount is spiritual pow-wow instead of spiritual power.

—The Christ of the Mount

In the surrender of ourselves we put ourselves at the disposal of the Spirit.

—The Way

My life motto: "Not able to do it, but enabled."

—Growing Spiritually

The Spirit will create a concern where others are unconcerned.

—The Way

Spirituality directed by wisdom is beneficial, but spirituality directed by ignorance is blighting. Some have the Spirit and no wisdom, and some have wisdom and no Spirit. Both alone are weak. Together they make the Christian.

—The Way

God gave us power to communicate with each other. Shall He not communicate with us?

—The Reconstruction of the Church

God kept on talking when His book had gone to press.

—The Way

Four steps in receiving and retaining the Holy Spirit: I must ask, I must receive by faith, I must give myself, and I must obey.

—The Way

Since perfect character is an attainment, it will take ages, but since perfect love is an obtainment, it need not take ages. But it will take the one thing we have—ourselves.

—*The Christ of the Mount*

Prayer: O living Spirit, I want my whole being to be redeemed. Thy work is in the area of the sub-conscious, an area I can't control. So I turn it over to Thee to cleanse and control and redirect. I thank Thee. Amen.

—*The Way*

Prayer: O Christ, I know that Thy distinctive baptism is the baptism of the Holy Spirit and power. I need inner reinforcement. Then give me this power that will change the whole level of life for me. In Thy name. Amen.

—*The Way*

Home

The only sickness is homesickness.

—*Song of Ascents*

This age is homesick for God. It is confused and empty and can't stand the emptiness. The head of a sorority said to me: "My generation is an uncommitted generation—the next generation will be committed to a mental institution."

—*The Reconstruction of the Church*

A strange nostalgia is upon humanity. Homesickness for God is responsible for most of our other sicknesses—mental, spiritual, physical, corporate.

—*The Way*

Being at home was to be in the will of God.

—*Song of Ascents*

We have tried to be at home away from Home.

—*The Way*

Our cosmic Home is the Kingdom of God.

—*The Way*

All coming to Christ has the feeling of homecoming upon it. All going away from Christ has the feeling of estrangement, of orphanage, of going away from home upon it.

—*Song of Ascents*

We laugh at the Boston woman who, when asked if she traveled, replied: "Why should I travel? I'm already here."

—*Song of Ascents*

People ask me where I live, and I have to reply: "In a suitcase."
—Song of Ascents

HUMANISM

I would glance at men and gaze at Jesus.
—Song of Ascents

This dethroning of the self-giving God and the enthroning of the self-seeking self as god is psychologically devastating. . . . Committed only to ourselves, the next generation will be committed to a mental institution.
—Song of Ascents

Jesus the Divine has aroused more interest in the unwanted of the world than all the humanists put together.
—The Reconstruction of the Church

The theology that begins anywhere and everywhere except Jesus Christ goes everywhere and gets nowhere. If you lose Jesus, you lose both Jesus and God. The result is a barren humanism.
—The Reconstruction of the Church

If you glance at Christ and gaze at men, it is sub-Christian.
—The Reconstruction of the Church

HUMILITY

One class and one class only will rule the future, the servants of all.
—The Reconstruction of the Church

The servant of all becomes the greatest of all.
—In Christ

Real humility is not rooted in a sense of humiliation; it is rooted in a sense of being inwardly great in Him.
—In Christ

Only those who are truly great can afford to be humble.
—Growing Spiritually

I was free from the vast complication of keeping up a position. I could go first class or third class—my values were elsewhere. I had to keep up nothing, for I wanted nothing.
—The Way

Those who act as if they don't have any needs have the most.
—Growing Spiritually

The great are not those who have the greatest number of servants, but those who serve the greatest number.
—Song of Ascents

"I've resigned as the General Manager of the Universe," said a young man in one of our Ashrams. So have I.

—*Song of Ascents*

I was on a plane, and the stewardess brought around a card asking: "What do you think of our meals?" I wrote: "Too good for a ransomed sinner."

—*Song of Ascents*

"I was wrong. I'm sorry. Forgive me." Those three sentences of only seven words are the most cleansing compound of words ever put together. It will cleanse any situation, any institution, any nation where it is sincerely uttered.

—*The Reconstruction of the Church*

If you won't be humble, you will be humbled.

—*The Way*

HUMOR

Laughter is a fine tonic. Don't bottle it.

—*Growing Spiritually*

A man said, "I prefer the east-west face, rather than the north-south face."

—*Growing Spiritually*

I passed a place in Los Angeles with this sign on it: "Jones Jolly Joint" and I laughed and said, "That's me—on the inside"; and I didn't have to attend a "joint" to be jolly.

—*Growing Spiritually*

"Why don't you get stomach ulcers from the unjust criticism you are constantly getting?" a pastor asked me. And I laughed and said, "Why, I've learned how to laugh."

—*Growing Spiritually*

When you get to taking yourself and life too seriously, deliberately go to the looking glass and burst out laughing. I often do it. It's contagious. The inside catches it.

—*Growing Spiritually*

Six years ago a little girl said to her mother: "How old is Stanley Jones?" When the mother replied that he was seventy-seven, the little girl replied: "Why, how can that be? He acts as though he is just beginning."

—*Song of Ascents*

Did Jesus ever laugh? Rufus Moseley replied, "Well, I don't know, but He certainly fixed me up so I could laugh."

—*Song of Ascents*

The art of laughing at yourself is the highest kind of laughter.

—Growing Spiritually

A missionary who was Irish and had a great sense of humor, stood looking at the sunset at the monsoon period with me at Sitapur. She said: "What a wonderful sunset—for such a little place!"

—Song of Ascents

Little girl's prayer: "God bless mama and papa, my brothers and sisters, and all my friends. And now, God, do take care of yourself, for if anything happened to you, we'd all be in the soup."

—Song of Ascents

IDOLATRY

An idol is a relative thing become an absolute.

—The Way

If you surrender to your self as god you won't like your god.

—Victory Through Surrender

This using of God to give us peace of mind and to make us healthy is a species of self-idolatry which is very prevalent and very popular—and very shallow.

—Growing Spiritually

The primary question is: What do you love supremely?

—Growing Spiritually

To make any rite, any ceremony, essential to salvation is to make an idol of it.

—The Way

The Church behind Christ is the greatest serving institution on earth; in front of Christ it is an idol. If it becomes an end in itself, it loses itself.

—The Way

When the secular tries to be an end in itself by saying that the secular is the sacred, then it is idolatry; for when a relative thing claims to be an absolute thing that is idolatry pure and simple.

—The Reconstruction of the Church

JEALOUSY

You can be jealous or lovable; you can't be both.

—The Way

Jealousy is poison. . . . Out of jealousy comes a whole brood of ugly evils.

—The Way

Joy

I wake up not with a groan, but with a grin.

—Song of Ascents

I won't get up tomorrow morning saying: "Stanley Jones, why were you a Christian last night? What made you do it?" I'll get up with a grin; some get up with a groan.

—Growing Spiritually

The Christian has more joy in the square inch than others have in the square mile.

—Growing Spiritually

It is fun to be a Christian.

—Song of Ascents

I saw a sign over a garage which specialized in repairing broken car springs, saying; "Limp in and leap out." That's what surrender of yourself and your sorrow and gloom to God will mean: you will limp in and you will leap out!

—Growing Spiritually

The Christian sings, and sings from the depths. He doesn't sing to make himself happy; he sings because he is profoundly happy.

—The Way

Happiness is dependent on happenings, and is therefore occasional; joy is dependent on relationship with Christ, and therefore permanent.

—In Christ

A minister once wrote me: "Thank you for putting my stars back in my sky—they had all gone out." Jesus does that. He puts our stars back in our skies and a song in our hearts and on our lips.

—Song of Ascents

Many of us hold truths, but they are "bed-ridden truths—they don't walk and dance and go in procession with banners waving.

—Growing Spiritually

A missionary lady was being taken out to be beheaded by bandits. On the way she thought how ridiculous it would be to see her head rolling down the hill and she in spirit going on to glory. So she burst out laughing. Her captors asked her what she was laughing about. She told them and then laughed. "Well," they said, "if it's going to make you happy, we are not going to do it." So they freed her. She laughed her way out of her own beheading.

—Song of Ascents

Rendel Harris says, "Joy is the strength of the people of God; it is their glory; it is their characteristic mark."

—*Growing Spiritually*

Someone has described Christian joy as the flag raised over the castle when the King is in residence.

—*In Christ*

We sing, not because we are worthy, but because He is worthy; we sing, not because of what we have done, but because of what He has done. "Worthy is the Lamb" is our theme song.

—*In Christ*

My joys are beyond the reach of sorrow, for the eternal joy has invaded me.

—*Growing Spiritually*

If there is no joy, there is no Christianity, for Christianity is joy.

—*Growing Spiritually*

It's fun to be eighty-three and a Christian, and it is getting funnier all the time.

—*Song of Ascents*

Christians sing—they have to or burst!

—*Growing Spiritually*

If we are not redeemed from unhappiness, we are not fully redeemed.

—*Growing Spiritually*

Someone asked a joyous modern saint if Jesus ever laughed and his reply was: "I don't know, but I do know that He has fixed me up so that I can laugh."

—*The Way*

We sing because our broken hearts have been mended, our broken lives remade. We sing because we are in Him—the Redeemer.

—*In Christ*

When I walked out into the world the morning after I made my self-surrender I thought I had never before seen the world; the trees clapped their hands and all nature was atingle with joy and beauty.

—*The Christ of the Mount*

Joy is a by-product of love. If you seek joy first, it will elude you. But if you go out to love everybody in the name of Jesus, joy will seek you out.

—*Growing Spiritually*

An hour spent in the presence of God brings the purest joy known to man.

—*The Way*

When I am in His will, life is not a struggle; it is a Song.

—*Song of Ascents*

I often ask an audience singing a joyous hymn in a melancholy way; "Are you happy?" and when they say, "Yes" I suggest that they notify their faces!

—*Growing Spiritually*

There is more joy in the square inch in Christ than there is in the square mile outside.

—*The Way*

Unless your song is cosmic, it is comic.

—*Song of Ascents*

Come to Him and be glad; go from Him and be sad.

—*In Christ*

JUDGMENT / HELL

Some people get results, others get consequences.

—*The Way*

The judgments of Christ and the judgments of life are the same. If you won't listen to the judgments of Christ, you will have to listen to the judgments of life.

—*The Way*

The hell of being bad is a bad hell.

—*The Way*

To be centered on your self is to be in hell—now.

—*Victory Through Surrender*

This modern age has put hell out of the door, but it has come back by the window. Dismissed from the universe it has moved inside us in the form of inner neuroses and conflicts.

—*The Way*

The saddest sad sight on this planet is a person who has had the desires of his heart but has found not fulfillment, but leanness of soul.

—*Growing Spiritually*

The past is not dead: it comes into the present as guilt.

—*Song of Ascents*

We once thought God threw people into the fires of hell. . . . The God revealed in Christ was different. Does that mean that hell has been abolished? By no means. It means that we are putting the responsibility for hell where it belongs—on us. . . . We light our own funeral pyre. . . . Sin and its punishment are one and the same thing.

—*In Christ*

The body is dust and to dust it will return. If our lives are invested in the physical side of our nature, then they will go to dust with it.

—The Christ of the Mount

Jesus is not on trial now. We judge ourselves by our judgment of Him.

—The Way

This moral universe has the last word, and that last word is the final word. We choose, but the moral universe decides the results of our choosing. . . . We must come to terms with the moral universe or get hurt.

—The Way

You are your own hell or your own heaven.

—The Way

Sin is hell begun. It is a state before it is a place. Anyone who is living in sin is living in hell now. You take that state of sin out with you into the next life, and you will get a place corresponding to the inner state. Hell is portable. God doesn't give it to you; you choose it.

—In Christ

Your self is your heaven or hell now.

—Victory Through Surrender

If any soul is lost, he will only be able to look within and say, "I am responsible."

—In Christ

KINDNESS

Speak well of your enemies for you made them.

—Growing Spiritually

Only by kindness can people be changed.

—Growing Spiritually

Without kindness there is no virtue in the other virtues.

—Growing Spiritually

If you won't be just, you can't be secure.

—Song of Ascents

Prayer: O Father, help me this day to do some little act of kindness that may live in somebody's memory forever. Amen.

—Growing Spiritually

"Treat one another with the same spirit as you experience in Christ Jesus" (Phil. 2:5). This is the high water of morality in this universe. Beyond this the human race will not, and cannot, progress.

—Growing Spiritually

Severe with self, generous and kind to everyone, especially the unkind and ungenerous.

—*Growing Spiritually*

Kingdom of God

We do not build the Kingdom—we receive it.

—*Song of Ascents*

The Kingdom of God will not come through you but as you.

—*Sat Tal Ashram wall mottoes*

The unshakable Kingdom is embodied in the unchanging Person. Not only absolute goodness looks out of His eyes, but absolute power.

—*Song of Ascents*

The Kingdom of God and the Holy Spirit are the two missing notes in much of our Christianity. And Jesus made both of them central—one the pattern, the other the power.

—*The Way*

Christ plus the Kingdom equals the Way.

—*The Way*

The Christian Way is the ground plan of the universe.

—*The Way*

Jesus was obsessed with the Kingdom of God. He used the phrase, or its equivalent, a hundred times.

—*Song of Ascents*

Men need nothing in these modern days so much as they need a working philosophy of life—an adequate way to live.

—*The Christ of the Mount*

The Kingdom: You enter it personally; you live in it corporately.

—*Song of Ascents*

What we call the Sermon on the Mount is the way a Christian will act. . . . It is his working philosophy of life.

—*The Christ of the Mount*

The Christian faith: It undertakes to do nothing less than replace the present unworkable world order with the Kingdom of God on earth, the most radical proposal ever presented to the mind and will of man.

—*The Reconstruction of the Church*

God not only redeems in terms of Jesus Christ. He rules in terms of Christ. I repeat: He is the Kingdom embodied and illustrated.

—*The Reconstruction of the Church*

Youth have three great decisions of life to make: (1) The choice of a life work. (2) The choice of a life partner. (3) The choice of a life philosophy. . . . The last should be first.

—*The Way*

The best introduction I ever received: "The significance of the speaker is not in himself, but in the cause with which he is identified—the Kingdom of God!" The perfect introduction. One could speak after that, for supreme values were supreme.

—*The Way*

[Philip] preached a new Order, the Kingdom of God, and the Person, Jesus. He combined in his message the necessity of an Order and a Person, a gospel for the whole life.

—*The Way*

[Barnabas] The test and sign of a real Christian is to rejoice in someone else's work. He was interested in the Kingdom, not in his part in that Kingdom.

—*The Way*

We cling to the little things in religion and miss this great thing—the central thing—the Kingdom.

—*The Way*

The conservatives emphasize the Person; the liberals emphasize the Order. But Philip put them together. So did Paul (Acts 28:31).

—*The Way*

My conviction is that the Kingdom of God is realism, the only realism; anything outside, or against, that Kingdom is unrealistic and doomed to failure.

—*Song of Ascents*

The Kingdom of God is Significance; all else is insignificance.

—*The Way*

Ultimately you can rejoice only in that which has ultimate significance.

—*The Way*

As the Apostles' Creed now stands you can accept every word of it and leave the essential self untouched. Suppose we had written it in our creeds. . . ."I believe in the Sermon on the Mount and in its way of life, and I intend, God helping me, to embody it!" . . . I feel sure that if this had been our main emphasis, the history of Christianity would have been different.

—*The Christ of the Mount*

Jesus is revealing the nature of reality. He is not only revealing the nature of God, He is revealing the nature of life.

—*The Way*

The Gospel of the Kingdom of God gives the real relationship between the secular and the sacred.

—*The Reconstruction of the Church*

Everything in the Kingdom is open to those who surrender to and obey the Kingdom.

—*The Way*

Any prayer or program or creed that does not put the Kingdom of God first is not a Christian prayer, a Christian program, or a Christian creed.

—*The Way*

Man needs nothing, absolutely nothing, so much as he needs to feel that he belongs to an unshakable kingdom — the Kingdom of God.

—*The Reconstruction of the Church*

The Christian faith . . . turns its redemptive energy into transforming the individual into perfection and into transforming the present world order into the Kingdom of God.

—*Growing Spiritually*

The only ultimately and finally real fact is the Kingdom of God.

—*Song of Ascents*

Everything is made in its inner structure to work in the Christian way. When it does, it works well; when it works some other way, it works its own ruin.

—*In Christ*

The Kingdom of God is within you—in your nerves, your tissues, your blood, your very make-up.

—*The Way*

"Fear not little flock; for it is your Father's good pleasure to give you the Kingdom." No more preposterous words could have been spoken—a handful of fishermen having a Kingdom!

—*Growing Spiritually*

All of my influence, all of my power, all of my self are at the disposal of the Kingdom—today.

—*The Way*

Nothing above the Kingdom, nothing against the Kingdom, everything for the Kingdom.

—*Growing Spiritually*

The Kingdom is Christlikeness universalized.

—*Song of Ascents*

The gradualistic gives me my task, and the apocalyptic gives me my hope.

—*The Way*

Help us this day as a group not merely to talk about the Kingdom of God but to BE the Kingdom of God.

—*The Way*

LAITY
THE PEOPLE OF GOD

The Christian movement is essentially a lay movement.

—*In Christ*

The Acts are called the Acts of the Apostles, but after the first few chapters the apostles drop out and the lay group takes over.

—*In Christ*

The word *laos*, from which the word laity is taken, literally means "the chosen people of God." A layman is a chosen person of God. . . . This makes his call as sacred as that of a clergyman.

—*In Christ*

If the laity lead they will produce leaders. If the laity only listen they will produce only listeners.

—*The Reconstruction of the Church*

Paul was a layman; no apostolic hands were laid on him.

—*In Christ*

The longest recorded sermon in the New Testament was given, not by any of the apostles, but by a layman—Stephen.

—*The Way*

All life must take on the sense of the sacred, and all callings be divine callings.

—*The Way*

Philip had such a mighty revival in Samaria that two apostles were sent down to regularize it! Laymen produced revivals which the ministers could not produce, but could regularize!

—*The Way*

A lay evangelist kept the apostles trotting to keep up with him.

—*The Way*

Jesus was a layman and had the lay mind—life was all of one piece. The apostles missed their step at this place and moved out of the line of succession of Jesus. The "apostolic succession" therefore is not Christian succession; it is the apostolic succession and they missed their step.

—*The Way*

The next great spiritual awakening is going to come through the laity.

—*The Reconstruction of the Church*

First century "informal missionaries"—Everyone who received the Gospel gave the Gospel.

—*The Reconstruction of the Church*

There is no especially sacred group or especially sacred calling; there are only sacred persons. Those persons are the "chosen" and sent, and that includes everyone who is in Christ.

—*In Christ*

I have been ordained by a bishop, the saintly Bishop Frank Warne, and I'm grateful for that ordination; but the mightiest ordination I've ever had was not by a bishop, but by a dying woman. When I stand up to preach, I can feel her hands on my head ordaining me to preach this gospel of joy.

—*Song of Ascents*

[Paul and Stephen] The two men who most clearly caught the essential elements of the Christian gospel were both laymen, outside the stream of "apostolic succession."

—*The Way*

Stephen was a deacon who became a beacon.

—*The Way*

We are discovering that the Christian movement was and is a lay movement. Jesus was a layman.

—*The Reconstruction of the Church*

[Paul the tent-maker] His interpretation of the Christian gospel was in life terms instead of lip terms. His Christianity walked.

—*The Way*

The sheer daring of telling a group of ex-fishermen on a hillside in a remote corner of the world that they were to become the one hope of the world! That they would save it from moral putrefaction and from moral darkness! It is breath-taking.

—*The Christ of the Mount*

The layman must now cut the cords that bind the Christian faith to an official priestly class and universalize it once again. They must give it back to the people of God, the laity.

—*The Reconstruction of the Church*

Lay witnessing is the key to the future.

—*The Reconstruction of the Church*

The laity, on the whole, have been in the stands as spectators, and the clergy have been on the field playing the game. . . the laity must come out of the stands as spectators and take the field as players; and the clergymen must come off the field as players and take the sidelines as coaches of a team.

—*The Reconstruction of the Church*

LAW
THE MORAL UNIVERSE

Jesus is as inescapable in the moral realm as the force of gravity is in the physical.

—*The Christ of the Mount*

Jesus has done the impossible about God—He has put strict moral qualities and lavish love together in the same Being.

—*The Christ of the Mount*

Anyone who thinks he can cheat a moral universe is a moral imbecile.

—*Growing Spiritually*

God has two hands: the hand of Grace and the hand of law. If you won't take from the hand of Grace, you must take from the hand of law.

—*The Way*

God's prohibitions are God's protections.

—*In Christ*

The more you discover the laws of your being, the more you discover the laws of God. They are the same. . . . The author of the laws of the Kingdom written in Scripture and the Author of the laws written in us is the same.

—*The Way*

Cling to the Rock, or break on the rocks.

—*The Way*

A little boy was found crying; when asked what was the matter, he replied: "I've been playing hookey from school all day, and I've just found out it is Saturday!" When we play hookey against the Kingdom of God we play hookey against ourselves.

—*Song of Ascents*

There are three possible attitudes toward reality. First, escape it. Second, rebel against it. Third, cooperate with it. The first two bring disaster; the third brings development. There is only one way to live—to cooperate with reality and get its resources behind you.

—*The Way*

Life is one and all laws that govern all life have one source—God.

—*The Way*

The earth and all it contains has a single law of its being, that law is the Kingdom of God. That law is the law of its life, the way life is made to work.

—*The Way*

The same moral laws that govern God's acting must govern ours. In other words, the moral laws are not rooted in the shifting customs of men, but they are rooted in the very nature of the Divine. This gives us a stable moral universe and it means that moral distinctions have ultimate meaning. Moral laws are not based on the divine will, but on the divine nature.

—*The Christ of the Mount*

We cannot break physical laws and not get hurt, nor can we break spiritual laws and not get hurt.

—*In Christ*

God's laws: they are not put there to bind our freedom; they are put there to save us from using our freedom to destroy ourselves.

—*The Way*

When Kant the philosopher said, "Two things strike me with awe: the starry heavens above and the moral law within," did he mean that the laws of those two worlds are equally dependable and equally authoritative and equally inescapable? Is there a way and not-the-way written in both?

—*The Way*

The universe is not indifferent to your virtue and your vice; it takes sides. It is a universe where you get results or consequences.

—*Song of Ascents*

You can't put your finger on a thing that is good that isn't Christian, and on anything Christian that isn't good.

—*The Way*

Mercy without righteousness is mushy.

—*The Christ of the Mount*

Life for the Pharisee was very complicated. For Jesus it was very simple. The Pharisee lived by innumerable taboos and regulations and laws. Jesus reduced these hundreds of laws to two: love to God and love to man. That is genius.

—*The Way*

The Jewish law limited revenge; Jesus abolished it.

—*The Christ of the Mount*

You do not break these laws written into the nature of things; you break yourself on them. These laws are class-blind, color-blind, race-blind, religion-blind; break them and you get broken. This is true of the individual and of the nation.

—*Song of Ascents*

LOVE, CHRISTIAN

A Christian is one who cares.

—*Sat Tal Ashram wall mottoes*

The acid test of my religion is the test of my relationships.

—*Growing Spiritually*

There are four levels of life: (1) The level of instinct; (2) The level of duty; (3) The level of receiving grace through faith; (4) The level of "faith working through love."

—*In Christ*

We can love people not for what they are, but for what we see they can be. And by our love we tend to produce the person we see—we love them into being.

—*Growing Spiritually*

The person who manifests love always becomes loveable—always.

—*The Way*

The church of the future must be the society of the caring, particular and universal caring.

—*The Reconstruction of the Church*

They had no God who cared, so they did not care.

—*Song of Ascents*

Some hold that we are abiding in Christ if we have correct views about Christ—if we are orthodox; some hold that we are abiding in Christ if we have correct conduct—if we are orthoprax. Neither of these, though both are important, is the supreme test. The supreme test is: Do I manifest love in all the manifestations of my life?

—*In Christ*

Christians are people who love people whom they do not like. They see in every person another person, the person he might become.

—*The Way*

The cup that is filled with sweetness will not spill bitterness no matter how hard it is knocked.

—*Growing Spiritually*

"Love never fails," for the giving out of love is the victory. If the person concerned accepts it, then you have won; if he does not accept it, you have also won, for you are the more loving.

—*Growing Spiritually*

The world is crying out for a society of unlimited caring.

—*The Reconstruction of the Church*

Love shall be first, last, and always my method.

—*Sat Tal Ashram wall mottoes*

Christianity—"The lamb is at the heart of the Throne"—self-giving, redeeming, sacrificial love is the center of power in the universe. That is the most startling thing ever announced about our universe. And the most important. If sacrificial love is at the heart of the throne, then sacrificial love must be at the heart of my motives. . . . if it isn't, then I'm at cross purposes with the throne—the final power.

—*Song of Ascents*

I have no enemies because I have no enmity.

—*The Way*

Perfect character is a growth, but perfect love is a gift.

—*The Christ of the Mount*

Happiness doesn't come to you; you join happiness on the way to doing something for others.

—*The Way*

Only the Christian society by its very nature provides the background of a caring God and a caring Redeemer, both of whom love their enemies. They overcome evil with good, hate by love, and the world by a cross. That produces the society of the caring.

—*The Reconstruction of the Church*

The love of Christ is the one and only thing which the devil cannot get into, for if he got into it he would cease to be the devil.

—*In Christ*

God has us hooked. If you don't love others as you love yourself, you can't get on with others, nor can you get on with yourself.

—*The Way*

He cleansed love from being *eros*—possessive love—and made it into *agape*—a non-possessive, sacrificial love.

—*In Christ*

Where other keys get jammed, love opens the door, for it fits the heart—every heart.

—*Growing Spiritually*

There is nothing love cannot face.

—*Sat Tal Ashram wall mottoes*

The highest statement of morality ever given on this planet of ours is this one: Treat one another with the same spirit as you experience in Christ Jesus" (Phil. 2:5).

—*Growing Spiritually*

The best definition I know of purity of heart is just here: a passion for righteousness and a compassion for men—this is purity of heart.

—*The Christ of the Mount*

Not how cultured, how rich, how educated, how high-born you are, but how much sacrificial love for others controls your being determines how high in the scale of existence you are.

—*Song of Ascents*

We don't try to love; we just let Love love.

—*Growing Spiritually*

You will give out love and only love, no matter what the other person gives out to you.

—*The Way*

Interesting people are always people who are interested.

—*The Way*

Communism doesn't love its enemies, it liquidates them, if possible.

—*The Reconstruction of the Church*

As I rose from my knees, I felt I wanted to put my arms around the world and share this with everybody. Little did I dream at that moment that I would spend the rest of my life literally trying to put my arms around the world to share this with everybody.

—*Song of Ascents*

If you love, you live; if you don't love, you don't live.

—*Growing Spiritually*

The love of God is the biggest thing in the universe, and when that love is incarnate in a deed, then the deed is big.

—*Growing Spiritually*

Love lightens all loads. Nothing is hard if done for love's sweet sake.

—*Growing Spiritually*

An African patient was puzzled because Dr. Albert Schweitzer was there: "Why did you come?" The doctor replied, "Jesus sent me." Where Jesus sends, the Spirit sways.

—*The Way*

It costs nothing but sentiment to love in general, but it really costs to love in particular.

—Growing Spiritually

Love is creative—it faiths faith out of the faithless, believes belief out of the beliefless, and loves love out of the loveless.

—Growing Spiritually

To be Christianized is to be sensitized.

—The Reconstruction of the Church

We do the highest because we love the Highest.

—The Way

Law touches the surface, love touches the center; one is retributive, the other is redemptive.

—The Christ of the Mount

I can now love myself safely and wisely, for I love something more than myself—God.

—Growing Spiritually

I shall take care of my motives. Then my actions will take care of themselves.

—The Way

Life is judged not by its accomplishments, but by its attitudes.

—The Christ of the Mount

Knowledge looks big, but it is big barrenness unless love is behind it.

—Growing Spiritually

There is no possible way to get rid of an enemy except to turn him into a friend, and there is no possible way to get rid of hate except by love.

—The Christ of the Mount

Go out today and find someone who needs your love, and give it and give it generously.

—Growing Spiritually

God had to wrap His Truth in Love and call His name Jesus.

—In Christ

Here everybody loves everybody.

—Sat Tal Ashram wall mottoes

A loveless knowledge is blind.

—In Christ

Marriage

Everything in the Lord, including marriage, is safe and secure. Everything outside the Lord is unsafe and insecure.

—In Christ

When our daughter was married, I wrote her: "I hope I shall never be in the way and never out of the way." I would be there when needed.

—*The Way*

I believe with Findlay and Dean Inge that the only honest thing for the church to do is to refuse to perform marriages except between its own members, or at least between those who are prepared to make an open confession of faith, and then to insist that the marriage thus entered into should be indissoluble except by death.

—*The Christ of the Mount*

It is better to remain single than to marry the wrong person.

—*The Way*

OBEDIENCE

We give ourselves tentatively to human orders; we give ourselves totally to the Divine Order.

—*The Way*

In a moral universe the only way to get more light is to act on the light you have.

—*The Way*

We know as much as we are willing to practice and no more.

—*Victory Through Surrender*

The initiation is His; the consent is ours.

—*Song of Ascents*

OLD AGE

Old age is just a new page upon which you can write life's noblest chapter.

—*Growing Spiritually*

Though the body is doomed to decay, the mind and spirit are not a part of that decay unless we allow them to be.

—*Growing Spiritually*

Sixty-four percent of the great achievements have been accomplished by persons who have passed their sixtieth year.

—*Growing Spiritually*

We have training courses on how to grow up, but not on how to grow old.

—*The Way*

Some in old age suffer from the hardening of the arteries, but more seriously from the hardening of the categories.

—*Victory Through Surrender*

Many of the happiest men and women in the world are those in their sixties, seventies, and eighties—happiest and most useful.

—The Way

Many men and women who have lived a life in the flesh, are reduced in after years to sniffing the empty bottles of their lusts as they try to live over again in memory their flesh life. It's a sorry spectacle. They took pleasure for joy, and pleasure lets them down—and how!

—Growing Spiritually

The saddest thing in life is to see a person come to the autumn time with nothing to show except a decadent self.

—The Way

Opportunity

Time is distilled opportunity. Don't waste it.

—The Way

Statistics show that after twenty-one the chances are three to one against becoming a Christian.

—The Way

Opposition to Christ

If you are on the Way you must get used to the sight of your own blood.

—The Way

Two kinds of opposition: cold steel or cold shoulder.

—The Reconstruction of the Church

Men hate to be disturbed—even for the better. The peacemakers must get used to the sight of their own blood.

—The Christ of the Mount

Peace

Peace comes from adjustment to reality, and there can be no adjustment to reality without adjustment to God.

—Growing Spiritually

If you look within you'll be discouraged; if you look around you'll be distracted; if you look back you'll be paralyzed; but if you look at Jesus you'll have peace.

—In Christ

You cannot have peace of mind unless you have something deeper than peace of mind.

—*Growing Spiritually*

POSSESSIONS

Tithing: Just as you give rental as an acknowledgment that the rented house belongs to another, so you give one-tenth as acknowledgment that the nine-tenths belongs to God.

—*Growing Spiritually*

God is the OWNER, and you are the ower. This puts God in His place and you in yours. You are not free to manage your material possessions as you like, but as He likes.

—*Growing Spiritually*

PRAYER

Prayer rewinds the springs of life.

—*The Way*

Prayer is not trying to bend God's will to my will; it is aligning my will to His will.

—*Song of Ascents*

Prayer creates the singing heart.

—*The Way*

If we know how to pray, we know how to live.

—*Growing Spiritually*

Someone has defined prayer: "To bring the whole of life into the light of God's presence for cleansing and decision—that is prayer." It is also power.

—*The Way*

Relaxed attention to God—that is prayer.

—*The Way*

Don't let the rest of the day decide this prayer time. Let this prayer time decide the rest of the day.

—*The Way*

If I pray, I'm like a bulb put into a socket—full of light and power; if I don't pray, then I'm like that same bulb pulled out of the socket—no light, no power.

—*Song of Ascents*

The poised prayerful heart is sure of its directions, is sure of its resources, and moves from task to task with calm confidence. The prayerless are hurried, flurried, worried.

—*The Way*

Prayer unties knots everywhere.

—*The Way*

To talk with God, no breath is lost—Talk on! To walk with God, no strength is lost—Walk on! to wait on go, no time is lost—Wait on!

—*The Way*

When man listens, God speaks; when man obeys, God acts . . . when man prays, God empowers.

—*Growing Spiritually*

My custom is to turn this early awakening around 3:30 or 4:00 into a Listening Post. I ask the Father: "Have you anything to say to me?" and in the quietness He tells me to correct this, that, and the other. It is all very quietly searching.

—*Growing Spiritually*

Prayer lets God's love in.

—*The Way*

Someone has defined education as change. Then prayer is life's deepest education, for in prayer you are being educated at the place that counts—at the center of your life.

—*The Way*

Jesus ran away from the crowds to pray. We run after the crowds—and don't pray.

—*The Way*

If you have to wait for anybody or anything, such as a train or an elevator, fill in that waiting time with prayer. That saves you from fretful frustration and makes your vacant spaces victorious spaces.

—*The Way*

Jesus was primarily prayer-conscious and secondarily crowd-conscious. He got both. We get neither.

—*The Way*

You do not have to overcome God's reluctance; you have to lay hold of God's highest willingness.

—*In Christ*

Someone wrote me: "I am an atheist, but the vision of Christians on their knees praying night and day for peace has touched me deeply."

—*Song of Ascents*

Pray in Jesus' name. That is, in His character. That is the sieve through which the unworthy prayers drop. The Christian prayers remain.

—*The Way*

In prayer you have a life transfusion. You are God-infused.

—*The Way*

We can make prayer a parade.
—*The Christ of the Mount*

Prayer brings the important to the center of consciousness and pushes the unimportant to the edges.
—*The Way*

Prayer is self-surrender—a blanket surrender of the self with no strings attached.
—*Song of Ascents*

Prayer is not trying to get God to do our will. It is getting our will into line with God's will.
—*The Way*

I know that when I pray I'm better, when I don't, I'm worse.
—*The Way*

Pray by the clock. If it starts being mechanical it will soon become medicinal—it will heal you at the heart.
—*The Way*

Prayer: O God, wake us up to Jesus. Give us His passion for prayer and His passion for people. May our needs drive us to Thee and the needs of others drive us to them. For we have discovered a working force. Amen.
—*The Way*

After you have prayed for others, ask if there are any "orders of the day" and then listen. God has purposes and plans He would unfold through you. Listen for specifications.
—*The Way*

Prayer is cooperation with God.
—*The Way*

Fall in love with God and you'll know what to say.
—*The Way*

In the heart of man—a cry; in the heart of God—supply.
—*The Way*

PREACHING

Melt people, don't maul them. It is easier to melt a block of ice than to break it up by smiting it with a hammer.
—*Growing Spiritually*

Today I shall not try to defend the faith, but illustrate it.
—*In Christ*

Share on the level of experience.
—*Song of Ascents*

If I ask people to obey, I must embody.
—*The Way*

All real preaching is testimony.

—*Song of Ascents*

Someone has defined a preacher as "one who preaches a whole gospel and wholly lives it."

—*The Way*

In the minutes of an old church in New England there was this entry: "A committee was appointed to examine the squeak in the pulpit." There are a lot of ministers who could answer that description—"a squeak in the pulpit." The real man of God is not a "squeak" but a Voice. He sounds out eternal verities in a positive way and produces positive results.

—*Growing Spiritually*

As a lawyer for God, putting up His case, I was a failure. As a witness for God, telling what He had done for me, I was a success. As in a flash I saw my calling: I was to be a witness.

—*Song of Ascents*

"Perhaps" preaching is a paralyzed preaching.

—*The Reconstruction of the Church*

Not a peddler of ecclesiastical wares, but a proclaimer of good news—Jesus!

—*In Christ*

Someone has defined a great deal of preaching as "a mild-mannered attempt by a mild-mannered parson to get mild-mannered people to become more mild-mannered."

—*Growing Spiritually*

I have an extraordinary subject, the good news of Jesus Christ.

—*Song of Ascents*

The Gospel is not good advice, but good news. It is not primarily teaching us how to live, but an offer of Life. Jesus did not come to show us the Way, but to show Himself as the Way.

—*The Way*

If we are in Christ, then we are not verbal defenders of the faith, but vital demonstrators. He Himself is His own defense. We show Him, and He defends Himself.

—*In Christ*

With good views but not good news . . . all verbal, but not vital.

—*Song of Ascents*

Philosophies and moralisms, however good they may be, are powerless to change character and life.

—*Song of Ascents*

When you hear some preachers you go away saying, "What a wonderful preacher," instead of saying, "What a wonderful Savior!"

—*In Christ*

Two preachers were being analyzed by two laymen. They came to this conclusion: "When one stands up to preach he preaches eloquently, but he is alone. When the other man stands up to preach, there isn't the eloquence, but the effect is astonishingly different. The reason is, now there are two."

—*The Way*

We can say the right thing with the wrong spirit.

—*In Christ*

We are "commissioned" to preach Jesus; nothing else is worth preaching, absolutely nothing.

—*In Christ*

If we are to speak with His emphasis we must saturate ourselves with the New Testament.

—*In Christ*

The Word is always bigger than our words.

—*In Christ*

Witnessing is more effective than preaching in winning others. Witnessing comes from the heart—preaching may come from the head. That which is to reach the heart must come from the heart.

—*In Christ*

When we speak in ourselves, from ourselves, and for ourselves we are peddlers of God's Word.

—*In Christ*

Our churches are often empty because the preacher is empty. Where the preacher finds, the pew fills.

—*The Way*

Paul could say, "This one thing I do." They can say, "These forty things I dabble in." Paul left a mark; they leave a blur.

—*Song of Ascents*

You get a hearing if you have a divine message, a human sympathy, and a life that illustrates the message.

—*The Way*

I have found that this is what people want to hear—testimony of what has happened and is happening to you.

—*Song of Ascents*

I had taken as a life motto that I would not preach what I was not experiencing.

—*Song of Ascents*

If we preach a philosophy—ideas about life, or a moralism . . . we do not become a "father in Christ Jesus"—we do not beget spiritual children. It is only "through the gospel" that we become creative.

—*In Christ*

When we listen to God, then people will listen to us.

—*Growing Spiritually*

Believe your beliefs and doubt your doubts, and don't speak unless you are voicing belief.

—*Growing Spiritually*

When a prisoner of Rome said to us: "They will listen," he uttered one of the truest words in history—and the most important (Acts 28:28).

—*The Reconstruction of the Church*

If the heart is empty, then deep does not speak to deep. Shallowness speaks to shallowness.

—*The Way*

We try to come out at His feet.

—*Song of Ascents*

A very able man, brilliant and learned, at the end of a series of addresses said: "Well, I hope I pricked some bubbles." His great abilities were dedicated to the pricking of bubbles. And when this was accomplished, what was left? A wet spot! And that was all.

—*Growing Spiritually*

The devil tempts us as ministers "to speak of many things," to try to be an oracle in matters outside our sphere. But we must resist and say, "This one thing I know" and then point to the Redeemer.

—*Growing Spiritually*

A reduced Christ is the same as a rejected Christ.

—*In Christ*

Someone asked a working woman why she went to hear a preacher who was noted for his thoughtful sermons and got this surprising reply: "He cleans out the gutters of my mind."

—*Growing Spiritually*

They tell us that a piece of steel is magnetized by setting all its molecules in harmony with each other. As long as the molecules are at cross purposes, there is no magnetism.

—*Growing Spiritually*

The minister cannot afford to let the group control him, but neither can he afford to refuse to let the group correct him.

—In Christ

The moment he gave her the gospel—the crucified and risen Savior—he became creative, the father of a newborn soul; he "got her in." The gospel is the redemptively creative activity of God.

—In Christ

We want to hear the man who has heard from God.

—Growing Spiritually

PSYCHIATRY

Pure psychoanalysis is basically self-defeating—it concentrates the patient on himself for a year or more. If he didn't have a neurosis at the beginning, he would probably have one at the end because of the self-preoccupation for a prolonged period. The disease is self-preoccupation.

—Song of Ascents

The pagan psychologist goes on the assumption that all that is needed is to have yourself analyzed; all else will follow. The outstanding psychology is psychoanalysis, not psychosynthesis. Some of the most disrupted people in the world are the analyzed. They are picked to pieces, but not put together again.

—The Way

RELIGIONS OF THE WORLD

A god who doesn't care doesn't count.

—Song of Ascents

Religion of itself is not necessarily a good thing.

—The Christ of the Mount

As long as man wants to live fully and better, he will be religious. We are incurably religious.

—Song of Ascents

Trace back the economic and social evils of the East and you will find almost every one of them rooted in religious custom.

—The Christ of the Mount

There is nothing more fallacious than saying, "Any faith is good, provided you are sincere." You may sincerely follow the wrong thing to a wrong destination.

—Growing Spiritually

Faith working through love can be and is the most beautiful thing in the world. Faith working without love can be and is the ugliest thing in the world. It has caused more havoc in the world than possibly any other one thing.

—*In Christ*

Oft times the rejection of religion is not because of the wickedness of men, but because of the worthlessness of religion.

—*The Christ of the Mount*

Mankind is looking for two things—a song to sing and a creed to believe.

—*In Christ*

I have lived all my life amid religions which, when they came to the business of life now, have tried to rise above it, have tried to step apart from it, have feigned indifference to it, have steeled themselves against it, have done everything except face it and solve it—"in."

—*In Christ*

Two schools of thought and attitude toward the Self—the school of self-realization and the school of self-renunciation.

—*Victory Through Surrender*

I say to people, and have said for fifty years and more, "If you can find God some other way, other than Christ, then go out and find Him and come back and tell me, and I will rejoice with you." No one has ever come back to report that he has found God.

—*Song of Ascents*

The non-Christian faiths never have believed in progress.

—*Growing Spiritually*

BUDDHISM

"Is there any existence in Nirvana?" I asked a Buddhist monk. "How can there be?" he replied. "There is no suffering in Nirvana, hence no existence." Buddha would get rid of the problems of the self by getting rid of the self. That is the most devastating answer ever given to the problem of the self. . . . This is spiritual hari-kari.

—*Victory Through Surrender*

Buddhism is based on pure pessimism about life: Life and suffering are one.

—*Growing Spiritually*

The first note of Buddha's teaching is Suffering; The first note that Jesus strikes is Joy.

—*The Christ of the Mount*

Buddha would get rid of the problems of life by getting rid of life. He would get rid of our headaches by getting rid or our heads. It was a vast "no."

—*The Reconstruction of the Church*

In Buddhist temples nuns sit on the floor back to back. It is all a quest of the alone for the Alone.

—*Song of Ascents*

CHRISTIANITY

Jesus cleansed the universe of the many gods and goddesses and gave us the one holy God, our Father. The gods of self-seeking adoration gave way to the God of self-giving sacrifice.

—*Victory Through Surrender*

In other religions we have man's search for God, in the Gospel we have God's search for man.

—*The Way*

We know that any truth, any goodness, or any beauty found in other cultures is a ray of "that Light which lighteth every man that cometh into the world. . . ." Christ has been there before us, though unrecognized and unknown

—*The Christ of the Mount*

There is nothing infallible in the Pope except that he's infallibly fallible like the rest of us.

—*Growing Spiritually*

Whenever real Christianity is operative, there hope is born and there hope flourishes.

—*Growing Spiritually*

Moses pointed to the Law; Mohammed to the Koran; Confucius to the Analects; Buddha to the Noble Eightfold Path. Only Jesus pointed to Himself: "Come to Me." No one less than divine dare do that without blasphemy.

—*The Reconstruction of the Church*

His voice sounds through the ages as the most awful challenge to all veneer, all seeming, all doublemindness, all unreality in religion.

—*The Christ of the Mount*

Jesus never used the term "religion," and never visualized what He was bringing as a religion to set alongside other religions . . . He is God's redemptive offer to man.

—*Song of Ascents*

There are many religions; there is but one Gospel.

—*Sat Tal Ashram wall mottoes*

"Realized in Christ Jesus"—that is the most decisive verse in religious literature. In all faiths, except in Jesus Christ, there is verbal anticipation; only in Jesus is there realization.

—*In Christ*

As I have listened to the finest that the religious East could produce I have been struck with the fact that outside of Christ men were uncertain, fumbling. In Christ they had found God, or rather, God had found them.

—*The Christ of the Mount*

The Stoic endures trouble; the Hindu accepts; the Mohammedan submits; the Buddhist takes it as inevitable; only the Christian exults in the midst of trouble. For he makes his troubles make him.

—*Growing Spiritually*

(There is) no namby-pamby talk of the equal worth of all religions in Christ. He is tender, but truthful; sympathetic, but severe.

—*The Christ of the Mount*

There are no "Hallelujah Choruses" in ancient or modern non-Christianity.

—*Song of Ascents*

The Christian faith is a universal faith, and at home in any given situation.

—*Song of Ascents*

As for those who lived before Christ, the answer is that nobody has ever lived before Christ. "Before Abraham was, I am." (John 8:58)

—*The Way*

Beyond Christ religion or moral progress does not go.

—*The Christ of the Mount*

All other faiths are philosophies or moralisms.

—*Song of Ascents*

The statement has been said so often that "all religions are basically alike" and that "all roads lead to God" that many have come to believe it. But to put the matter under life to get the verdict of life itself tells another story. The results are not the same. When Jesus said, "I am the Way," life agreed.

—*Song of Ascents*

Put out the candles, the Sun has come up!

—*Victory Through Surrender*

HINDUISM

In India the worshiper goes, for the most part, to the temple to worship alone, not for corporate worship.

—*Song of Ascents*

When the Hindu meditates, he doesn't meditate on God, but meditates on himself as God. "Aham Brahm"—"I am Brahman"—is the inner refrain. It is a refrain, but not a realization. Life doesn't back it.

—*Song of Ascents*

I have seen across the years in India numerous attempts "to impose divine qualities upon the framework of human nature," and they have all literally produced monstrosities or absurdities.

—*Song of Ascents*

A thoughtful Hindu editor summed it up for me in this way: "Hinduism is God without morality; Buddhism is morality without God; Christianity is God with morality."

—*The Christ of the Mount*

Religion among the Greeks and among the Hindus lacks moral basis. Someone has called our attention to the fact that there is not a villain in the *Iliad*—there wasn't sufficiently developed moral sense to create a villain as moral distinctions didn't matter.

—*The Christ of the Mount*

Karma is the nerve-center of Hinduism and the cross is the nerve-center of Christianity. In karma you reap what you sow, there is no forgiveness; in the cross we reap forgiveness by the act of God.

—*The Reconstruction of the Church*

Reincarnation: Belief in rebirth is no hopeful hypothesis, for the originators of rebirth, the Hindus, say you must go through 82 million rebirths before you are released from its weary round. Could anything be more hopeless and barren? Salvation to the Hindus means salvation from rebirth.

—*The Reconstruction of the Church*

Reincarnation: There is a valid and vital alternative for rebirth, and that is new birth in this birth.

—*The Reconstruction of the Church*

Hindu: They were seeking not communion with God, but union with God—seeking realization that they are God. Life doesn't back the idea that man is God.

—*Song of Ascents*

I find the Hindus of India say more than anything else in any discussion of religion: "Well, all religions are the same. All roads lead to the top of the mountain. All lead to God." This is a statement, not testimony. Life says something else, and what it says is exactly what this Scripture says: "He who has the Son has life; he who has not the Son has not life" (1 John 5:11-12).

—*In Christ*

A great Hindu philosopher was right . . . "There is only one who is worthy . . . Jesus Christ."

—*Song of Ascents*

ISLAM

Islam believes in smashing your enemies. It succeeded for a while, and then the sterility of an eye for an eye and a tooth for a tooth set in; a sterile civilization resulted.

—*Growing Spiritually*

Mohammedanism finds a desert or makes one; Christ finds a desert and makes it blossom like the rose.

—*The Way*

The Mohammedan faith is a very definite and strong faith, but for the most part it works without love and in doing so works havoc.

—*In Christ*

RESENTMENTS

You chew your own tongue when you chew on resentment.

—*Growing Spiritually*

A resentful heart is a restricted heart.

—*Growing Spiritually*

Take heed to yourself at a particular moment—at the moment when your brother sins against you. For your reaction to what he does to you may color and determine your whole life for good or ill.

—*Growing Spiritually*

Of all the things that choke and poison spiritual growth, resentments, justified or unjustified, are probably the most devastatingly effective.

—*Growing Spiritually*

If you take the method of retaliation, you call in a spirit that takes control of the situation and you will pass under its dominance.

—*The Christ of the Mount*

Don't fight resentments; surrender them.

—The Way

If my reactions are to be Christian, my repentance must be Christian.

—Growing Spiritually

RESPONSIBILITY

Not my responsibility, but my response to His ability.

—Song of Ascents

I have no responsibility except to live in union with God.

—The Way

RESURRECTION

Jesus didn't conduct funerals—He conducted resurrections!

—The Way

Lo—the Sunrise! He is Risen!

—The Way

Resurrection is inherent—in the seed, in Jesus, in me.

—The Way

He carries the Resurrection; the Resurrection doesn't carry Him. I believe in it because of Him.

—The Way

It is founded, not on a belief, but upon a demonstration—the resurrection of Jesus from the dead. Jesus not only proclaimed life after death; He demonstrated life after death.

—The Way

Before Jesus rose from the tomb, over the portals of death was written, "Nothing Beyond"; after He arose, it had to be written "Everything Beyond."

—Growing Spiritually

This, that I have in Jesus, does not have the feel of a funeral upon it; it has the feel of a resurrection.

—Song of Ascents

"They imagined she was going to wail at the tomb" (John 11:31). They could see nothing to be done except that—wail at a tomb, the picture of hopeless despair. But Mary did not go to a tomb. She went to a Person. and that Person knew what to say: "I am the resurrection and the life." Christ was the answer.

—The Way

Easter morning the mists cleared, and the world got the full message, "Jesus defeated death!"

—The Way

It is a part of the redemption of Christ to redeem the body as well.

—*Growing Spiritually*

I shall salute the resurrection of my body as an old friend: "I've known you all of my life. For life has been one long glorious resurrection. Welcome, friend, I knew you would come."

—*Song of Ascents*

I live in a resurrected Christ. Since He cannot die, neither can I.

—*The Way*

Earth's blackest day and earth's brightest day are only three days apart.

—*The Way*

Our crowning reason for believing in immortality: The best Man who ever lived on this planet believed in it, practiced it, demonstrated it, and proclaimed it.

—*The Way*

(The early disciples) are radiant and irresistible. They laugh their way through persecution, sing their way through prisons, and smile their way through death. For what? A hoax? Well, hoaxes don't produce hallelujahs, nor does body snatching produce transformed lives.

—*The Way*

Riches, Eternal

When you belong to Christ everything belongs to you.

—*Victory Through Surrender*

From nothing I was led into His everything.

—*Song of Ascents*

Those who really believe in and experience immortal life have life heightened, cleansed, dignified, and value-imbued.

—*The Way*

The whole of the Christian faith reduced to six words: "You are Mine; Life is yours!"

—*Song of Ascents*

When a future life is not believed in, present life becomes cheapened and its moralities undermined.

—*The Way*

In giving up things for Christ I gave up nothing but what subtracted from me, and when I got Him, I got everything that added to me.

—*The Way*

No past can inhibit my glorious present and my more glorious future.

—*Growing Spiritually*

Darwin was in search of origins; we are interested in destinations. He wrote the *Origin of the Species*, and we point to the "Destination of the Species."

—*The Way*

Truth by its nature is also eternal, for if it isn't valid everywhere, for all time, it isn't valid anywhere at any time.

—*The Way*

When I'm tempted to want this or that, I say to myself: "What you have is too good for a ransomed sinner." Then I laugh—laugh at the wonder of what I have.

—*Song of Ascents*

A Christian: he deserves nothing and has everything.

—*Song of Ascents*

Goodness has eternal meaning and cannot die.

—*The Way*

Will we know each other in the immortal world? The answer is: Will we be less intelligent than we are now? Know each other? We shall know each other perfectly, love each other deeply, and enjoy each other wholly.

—*The Way*

Self-surrender is the open door to God's everything.

—*Victory Through Surrender*

SALVATION

There is a door out of emptiness and futility, and that door is Jesus—the only Door I know. . . . When sin goes the condemnation goes. . . . What He has, He saves.

—*In Christ*

You cannot call Him Savior unless you call Him Lord. He saves those whom He owns—no others.

—*In Christ*

Christ and Christ alone is necessary to salvation.

—*In Christ*

[Soldiers loading on a train at railway station] Someone called out, "Boys, give them hell!" A father called out to his son, "Son, give them Christ!" That is the alternative: Christ or hell.

—*Song of Ascents*

There are some who say that "salvation is by character." We do not accept that. Salvation is by grace, through faith—salvation is by Christ.

—*The Way*

Salvation is not a mere transferring us from earth to heaven, but a transference from what we are to what He is—it is to be in Him.

—*In Christ*

Your very life depends upon being able to receive.

—*Growing Spiritually*

He was identified with us that we might be identified with Him. He shared what was in man that we might share what is in Christ.

—*In Christ*

The Christian faith believes and starts from the stating point of redemption. We need redemption not only from our worst sins and corruption, but from our best—from our wisdom, our righteousness, and our sanctification.

—*In Christ*

The center of Christian redemption is to save you from yourself.

—*Growing Spiritually*

Salvation that is not present is not salvation—it is only a hope.

—*In Christ*

We are not to imitate Him in life we are to receive Him as life.

—*In Christ*

Belonging to a group does not save me. Belonging to Christ does.

—*The Way*

If He isn't the Way there is no way.

—*In Christ*

Science

There is nothing in the teachings of Christ which the subsequent growth of human knowledge will render obsolete.

—*The Christ of the Mount*

What Jesus said in history became true in experience.

—*Song of Ascents*

Whichever way you approach life, from the Christian revelation down to life, or from science up through the facts, you come out at the same place.

—*The Way*

The most beautiful thing about modern science is not its discoveries, great as they are, but its attitude of mind, its love of truth, of frankness, its preciseness of vocabulary, its humility and willingness to follow the facts wherever they may lead.

—*The Christ of the Mount*

Science is working up through the facts to the Fact, through truths to the Truth.

—*The Way*

The highest degree of certainty would come where the two kinds of reality—the objective and the subjective—would come together, dovetail, speak the same thing, and thus corroborate each other. That happens in the Christian faith.

—*Song of Ascents*

What Jesus is saying is this: "Try all the ways of life you may, and in the end you will find that nothing comes out as solid reality but this way of mine. Everything else is sand; this way is rock." This is breath-taking.

—*The Christ of the Mount*

I think Jesus would say to the modern scientist who has a spirit of humility and love of truth, "Thou art not far from the Kingdom of God."

—*The Christ of the Mount*

Science comes to a violin solo and explains it in strictly scientific terms, but not very elegant ones: "A violin solo is the scraping of a horse's tail across the guts of a dead cat." But the violinist would probably object: "There are meanings and values which are using the structure of the violin; they cannot be weighed and measured."

—*Song of Ascents*

SELF-CENTEREDNESS

The self-centered are the self-disrupted.

—*The Way*

The center of our problems—the unsurrendered ego.

—*Growing Spiritually*

The self was never intended to be the center of the universe.

—*Victory Through Surrender*

Someone has said that there are Seven Deadly Sins: the first is dishonesty, and the other six are selfishness. But dishonesty too is a species of selfishness, so the seven are one—self-centeredness.

—*The Way*

Nietzsche died in a madhouse and the world that followed him went to the brink of hell in the last war—a natural outcome of the self-assertive attitude. Its genesis is selfishness, and its exodus is suicide.

—*The Christ of the Mount*

Nietzsche said: "Assert yourself." Here is the cult of self-expression.

—The Christ of the Mount

When you try to digest self-centeredness the stomach turns sour. You are not made to be the center of your universe.

—Victory Through Surrender

They tell us that cancer cells are cells that have turned selfish, they have ceased to serve the rest of the body and demand that the rest serve them.

—The Christ of the Mount

If you make self-centeredness your driving urge . . . you will be allergic to yourself.

—The Way

The two most important questions about a life: "What is your center?" and, "What is your circumference?"

—The Way

Anything that leaves you centered on yourself is off-center. . . . All the cults that talk about self-realization, self-cultivation, self-development, all the answers in the self . . . are doomed to ultimate sterility and death.

—In Christ

Some people never become mature. They are always adolescent, always insisting on their rights, their places, their selves at the center of the picture. They may be sixteen or sixty, but they have never grown up.

—The Way

The self-centered blame their problems on others.

—Victory Through Surrender

The first thing Jesus struck at in opening His Sermon was self-centered self-sufficiency (Matt. 5:3).

—Growing Spiritually

If you are on the verge of a nervous break, you are centered on yourself. The only way to break the downward slide is to go and get interested in and love someone other than yourself.

—Growing Spiritually

You can only know yourself in relation to your Heavenly Father.

—Victory Through Surrender

The Self-realization cults always spell the self with a capital *S*, meaning you are to realize your self as God. . . . It is an illusion. The self is created, a creature, and can never become the Creator.

—Victory Through Surrender

Someone asked the head of a mental institution: "I suppose these people in here are beside themselves?" "Oh no," he replied, "they are very much themselves. They don't think of a thing except themselves. They are pickled in themselves. That's why they are here."

—Victory Through Surrender

If the self is unhealed, unadjusted, out of place, then life as a whole is unhealed, unadjusted, out of place.

—Victory Through Surrender

Center yourself on yourself and you won't like yourself.

—Victory Through Surrender

Modern hedonism is summed up in the last words of an actor: "Let down the curtain, the farce is done!" Bertrand Russell said: "Doom falls upon a man, pitiless and dark!"

—Victory Through Surrender

If you are gloomy, then don't look around for the cause; look within.

—Growing Spiritually

Every self-centered person—religious or otherwise—is a declining, decaying person.

—In Christ

When I think only of myself I produce a war—within myself.

—The Way

Touch him and he is still touchy! The self is still there watchful of its own place and power and becomes the morbid center of spiritual problems.

—The Christ of the Mount

The most absolutely happy people of the world are those who choose to care till it hurts. The most miserable people are those who center upon themselves and deliberately shun the cares of others in the interest of their own happiness.

—The Christ of the Mount

The self-centered make themselves tired.

—The Way

The self doesn't know itself because it doesn't know God.

—Victory Through Surrender

If you try for self-realization, you will be centered on the "self." You will save your life and lose it.

—Song of Ascents

Self-centeredness produces disease.

—The Way

The strangest thing on this planet is our fear of surrendering to the one safe place in the universe—God.

—*Growing Spiritually*

You are out of Christ if the self is on the throne of your life, no matter how religious you may be.

—*In Christ*

If you do not have faith, you become cynical; and if you do not have love, you become self-centered; and if you are cynical and self-centered, you are on the road to inner disruption.

—*Growing Spiritually*

A great many people talk about self-expression who have no self to express. They have inward chaos and call it a self.

—*The Christ of the Mount*

Nervous breakdowns come from what? Too much thinking about them will produce them. A famous preacher delivered ten consecutive sermons on how to avoid a nervous breakdown and ended up with one! Whatever gets your attention gets you.

—*The Way*

Self-centeredness produces a self you cannot live with.

—*The Way*

The end is not to know yourself, but to know God.

—*The Reconstruction of the Church*

The biggest tragedy is to get your heart's desire if you get it in lieu of God's desire for you.

—*Growing Spiritually*

If you have a wrong mental map of your self, you will probably come to wrong landings, a disaster instead of a destination.

—*Victory Through Surrender*

Paul presented his Master and forgot himself, so we cannot forget Paul. He forgot himself into immortality. Many of us remember ourselves into oblivion.

—*In Christ*

By no known process can the self be eliminated. It is part of us . . . it is us! Put the self out of the door, it will come back by the window, usually dressed in religious garments, but the same self still.

—*Victory Through Surrender*

The self-centered are trying to live in an impossible way, namely, as though they are the center of the universe, and they are not. God is.

—*The Way*

The center of our problem is ourselves. The center of Christ's redemption is to save us from ourselves. If we are not saved from ourselves, we are not saved.

—*The Way*

I say "unsurrendered ego," not the ego. I am sure that the ego is God-created and as such is God-approved and is to be developed. It is not to be canceled or suppressed; it is to be expressed in God's ways.

—*Growing Spiritually*

O Christ, when life is centered in Thee it is fruitful; when it is centered in me it is frustrated.

—*The Way*

SELF-PITY

A self-pitying self is a pitiful self.

—*The Way*

If you have lost a loved one, don't lose the beauty of that love by corroding it with a morbid self-pity. That makes you lose the loved one and the love

—*Growing Spiritually*

Give others sunshine. Tell Jesus the rest.

—*Growing Spiritually*

If you've been looking at the hole in the doughnut, look at the doughnut.

—*Growing Spiritually*

SELF-SURRENDER

I have Jesus and He has me.

—*Song of Ascents*

Not who you are but whose you are.

—*Sat Tal Ashram wall mottoes*

Apart from self-surrender all our other surrenders to God are marginal and unimportant.

—*Song of Ascents*

We are to hand back to God the self that is handed to us by the Creator; to surrender the one and only thing we own.

—*Victory Through Surrender*

You belong to Another. He decides your life plans; He directs the details; He is the source of your power, for He is the center of your affections and loyalty.

—*Growing Spiritually*

The saint is not one who tries hard to be good, but one who surrenders to Goodness.

—*In Christ*

When I strut, I stumble; when I surrender, I succeed.

—*Growing Spiritually*

We never live until we have gone to our own funeral.

—*Victory Through Surrender*

The Christian faith is radical, for it goes to the root of all our problems, individual and collective, and deals with the unsurrendered self by self-surrender. It is therefore the one true physician of the soul. All else is tinkering.

—*Victory Through Surrender*

To me, the center of Christ's teaching: "He that saves his life shall lose it and he that loses his life shall find it."

—*The Christ of the Mount*

God can give power only to surrendered souls who have come to an end of themselves. Any other kind of spiritual power is spiritual powwow, verbal instead of vital.

—*The Way*

Jesus asks us to give the only possession we have—ourselves.

—*The Christ of the Mount*

Do not struggle and try, but surrender and trust and obey.

—*The Way*

The self in your own hands is a problem and a pain; in the hands of God it is a power and a possibility.

—*Victory Through Surrender*

The renounced and the serving are combined and become the meek, who shall finally inherit the earth.

—*The Christ of the Mount*

In self-realization you try to realize yourself, for all the answers are in you. In self-surrender you surrender yourself to Jesus Christ, for all the answers are in Him. One leaves you centered on you—a self-centered and self-preoccupied person, albeit a religious person. The other loses his self and finds it. For self-realization comes only through self-surrender.

—*Victory Through Surrender*

To have myself on my own hands is hell; to have myself in God's hands is heaven.

—*The Way*

His way is my way, and when I do not take His way I'm beside myself, less than myself, against myself. I cannot revolt against Him without revolting against myself.

—*In Christ*

Every man must go to his own funeral before he can sing the "Hallelujah Chorus."

—Song of Ascents

Amazing authority and power come to the self-surrendered.

—Growing Spiritually

Trying to cultivate the spiritual life around an unsurrendered self is like trying to keep healthy around a malignant cancer.

—Song of Ascents

The unsurrendered are the unreleased. They are tied up until they let go of themselves.

—Growing Spiritually

This law of saving your life by losing it is not based on God's whim, nor even on God's will—it is based on God's character. That is the way God is, and that is the way God acts. . . . He gave Himself.

—Victory Through Surrender

If He gives Himself, then I must give myself.

—The Way

A man spoke to God through an echoing barn, "I want more of You," and got back the reply, "I want more of you."

—In Christ

What happens when the self is surrendered to God? Does He wipe it out, or wipe it clean? He wipes it clean of selfishness. . . . Having cleansed us from our central selfishness He gives the self back to itself.

—Victory Through Surrender

To be a Christian is to belong to Jesus Christ by surrender to Him and obedience to Him.

—Song of Ascents

Hell turns to heaven on the turnstile of self-surrender.

—Victory Through Surrender

Until we let self go we are trifling with this business of being a Christian.

—Victory Through Surrender

Every unit—individual, group, nation—must surrender itself to save itself.

—The Way

Suppose two people intending to form a union in marriage should say: "We will have a union, but neither of us will surrender any sovereignty to the union." How long would the union last? About as long as many marriages now last, and for the same reason.

—The Way

We are at the feet of the God who washed our feet!

—*In Christ*

You supply willingness and He supplies the power.

—*Victory Through Surrender*

Everything belongs to me because I belong to Him.

—*In Christ*

The renounced in spirit gain the Kingdom of Heaven, the mourners gain the kingdom of inner comfort, the meek gain the earth. So the world above, the world within, and the world around belong to this man!

—*The Christ of the Mount*

We are "called to belong to Jesus Christ" (Rom. 1:6).

—*In Christ*

The principle and practice of self-surrender, self-losing to self-finding is inherent in God and in man.

—*Victory Through Surrender*

This possibility of firsthand, saving contact with God through and in Christ is open to all, from the dregs of humanity to the highest moralist on the same terms—surrender!

—*In Christ*

You can know yourself, can accept yourself, and can express yourself if you surrender yourself. No other way works.

—*Victory Through Surrender*

Self-surrender means more than denying yourself this thing, and leaving the self intact; it is a fundamental change of ownership. Self-denial usually has been watered down until it means little more than doing without luxuries. When Jesus used the phrase "let him deny himself," it literally meant, "utterly reject himself" or, "lose sight of himself."

—*Growing Spiritually*

You cannot discipline or cultivate a self which is off-center. The center must be changed to Christ by surrender.

—*Victory Through Surrender*

If you don't surrender to God, you have to surrender to emptiness, to despair, to a life of unhappiness.

—*Victory Through Surrender*

All that pessimism about life and yourself and others drops away when you surrender to God. You have faith and faith has you!

—*Victory Through Surrender*

To be sure that everything is covered, tell God you surrender all you know and all you don't know.

—The Way

For the Christian there is one responsibility and only one responsibility—to keep in union with God. When that union with God is intact, everything flows from it.

—The Way

A young man came to our Ashram and said: "I've resigned as the general manager of the universe!"

—Victory Through Surrender

The Christian life is not a struggle; it is a surrender.

—In Christ

I'm not striving to be good; I'm surrendered to Goodness.

—Song of Ascents

In self-surrender you are not doing something that is a marginal act in the universe, you are doing the central thing which this universe holds and demands—self-surrender.

—Victory Through Surrender

You cannot love God unless you surrender to God.

—Growing Spiritually

Solve the problem of the unsurrendered self, and you usually solve all the problems down the line.

—Song of Ascents

We do not say that self-surrender solves all our problems. That depends on the follow-through and the carrying out of its implications. But what it does do is to set up right relationships between you and God, you and yourself, and between you and others. It gives you a framework and an attitude in which your problems can be worked out . . . You have the central problem solved—the self is no longer the center trying to be God.

—Victory Through Surrender

This daily and hourly continual surrender saves you from the psychiatrist's couch where you have to unburden yourself through torturous months and years of piled-up problems, resentments, fears, self-preoccupation, and guilts buried in the subconscious.

—Victory Through Surrender

The sense of not belonging to anything real and eternal is the central insecurity of our time.

—Victory Through Surrender

A half-given self is a wholly divided self. None of that for me.

—*Growing Spiritually*

I have one concern and only one—that I be His.

—*Victory Through Surrender*

We often think the alternative is: To be His, or to be my own? If you are not His, however, you are not your own. If you lose Life, you lose life.

—*In Christ*

The love of God invades me, the peace of God pervades me, the will of God persuades me, and I am wholly His.

—*Growing Spiritually*

Life in our hands is life on our hands—a problem. Life in the hands of Jesus is no longer a problem; it is a possibility.

—*The Way*

Until you are surrendered you are a "self-ian"; when you are surrendered you are a "Christ-ian."

—*Victory Through Surrender*

If you won't live in harmony with God, you can't live in harmony with yourself.

—*Growing Spiritually*

Today I shall not struggle and try, but surrender and trust.

—*In Christ*

Not my responsibility, but my response to His ability.

—*In Christ*

I've come back from my own funeral. I'm alive in the Alive!

—*Song of Ascents*

You cannot ask Christ to walk into an unsurrendered ego.

—*In Christ*

Self-indulgence leads to self-exhaustion, and self-exhaustion leads to self-surrender, and self-surrender leads to self-control, and self-control leads to self-realization.

—*Growing Spiritually*

Nothing will be denied the man who denies himself.

—*The Christ of the Mount*

Prayer: O God, Thou art teaching us that the only way to find life is to lose it—to lose it in something beyond ourselves. Teach us the supreme lesson of losing our individual and our national selves in Thy Kingdom. Then we shall find ourselves—fulfilled. Amen.

In self-surrender you are fulfilling the very thing for which Christ died (2 Cor. 5:15).

—*Victory Through Surrender*

SIN

Sin is sour business.

—*Song of Ascents*

Sin is the Eternal Ugliness. Bad could never be beautiful.

—*The Way*

The greatest illusion, barring none, is that man can sin and get away with it.

—*In Christ*

"Evil" is the word "live" spelled backwards. It is an attempt to live life against itself.

—*Victory Through Surrender*

Sin and its punishment are one and the same thing. By its very nature it is disruptive.

—*The Way*

All the fruit of sin is either green or rotten—it is never just right.

—*The Way*

Sin and death—they are Siamese twins. Where you have sin you have death.

—*In Christ*

We are allergic to sin.

—*The Way*

The inane stupidity and dullness of evil makes its devotees invent more and more extremes to get the same result. It is under the law of decreasing returns.

—*The Way*

The Christian way is the natural way—the way we are made to live. . . . Sin is not natural, sin blights. It is sand in the machinery of life.

—*The Way*

If I run away from God I run away from all that is in God and am left with all that is in myself—emptiness.

—*In Christ*

"Oh, hell!" cries many a modern youth—and he thinks he is swearing. What he is doing is revealing expended resources within, and that he is living in the hell of the insufferable inane. He has gained the kingdom of rot.

—*The Christ of the Mount*

Sex is a dedication or a desecration, and when it becomes a desecration it becomes a degradation.

—*Growing Spiritually*

A college student: "I'd like this older generation to get acquainted with this guy called 'Kick'—he's a wonderful guy—gives you thrills." I felt like replying, Young man, may I suggest that you get acquainted with another guy called "Kick-Back." He's always a little behind the first guy and always has the last kick!

—*The Way*

Sin and sadness are one and the same thing.

—*The Reconstruction of the Church*

As dirt is matter out of place, so sin is the self out of place . . . making itself God.

—*Growing Spiritually*

Jesus: Here not only was the act of adultery forbidden, but the thought of adultery was also forbidden; adultery was set back from the deed to the thought.

—*Song of Ascents*

She had known God once and then had deliberately sacrificed her spiritual birthright for a mess of physical porridge—sexual freedom. She had grasped at the lurid colors of the sunset, and lo, all she had was the dark.

—*The Way*

Our natural urges are given to sustain us, but if they get out of place they can strangle us.

—*The Way*

What of those professing to follow Jesus who advocate the legitimacy of sexual intercourse outside marriage? They must give up Jesus or give up their advocacy of immorality.

—*Song of Ascents*

The battle of life cannot rise higher than the sexual battle. Lose here and you lose all down the battleline of life.

—*The Christ of the Mount*

Sin is self-consuming. It burns itself up. That is not something imposed on life by an angry God. That is something that is inherent in the moral universe.

—*In Christ*

Thrills ends with "ills."

—*The Way*

Those who are freest in sex get most tied up.

—*The Way*

Man is so fallen that he thinks that the laws of his being revealed in Christ are a foreign imposition.

—*Growing Spiritually*

Inevitably lust equals disgust.
—*The Way*

At the center of our wisdom, our righteousness, and our sanctification is the unsurrendered ego which keeps intruding into our wisdom and making it a strutting egoism; into our righteousness making it a bad-smelling self-righteousness; into our sanctification making it uninviting sanctimoniousness.
—*In Christ*

Evil is good prostituted.
—*The Way*

All our virtues need to be redeemed.
—*In Christ*

Self-love, the natural, can become selfishness, the unnatural. Self-respect, the natural can be allured into pride, the unnatural. Love, the natural, can be beguiled into lust, the unnatural. If they become god, become ends in themselves, then there is one result, Death.
—*The Way*

Evil is always complex, roundabout, tangled. Goodness is always a reduction of life to simplicity.
—*The Way*

What is in my mind today as meditation will come out of my life as fact.
—*Growing Spiritually*

Hold nothing in your mind that you do not want to hold within you permanently.
—*Growing Spiritually*

The goodness or badness of an act is determined by what it does to you. Does it lower or heighten the moral and spiritual you?
—*Growing Spiritually*

Do not let the light that is within you be given a twist so that your virtues become vicious, and your doctrines become deadly.
—*The Christ of the Mount*

To lie, to steal, to commit adultery, to get revenge on enemies, to criticize others, all these are sweet to the taste, but they are bitter to digest. The soul rejects them, for the soul and evil are allergic to each other.
—*Growing Spiritually*

Carlyle once said, "Sin is, has been, and ever shall be the parent of misery." And the central sin is the sin of trying to make your self God.
—*Victory Through Surrender*

The modern attempt is to have quantity of life at the circumference regardless of the quality of life at the center.

—The Christ of the Mount

Self-redemption is self-deception.

—In Christ

Self-rule equals self-ruin.

—The Way

If you tell a lie, you become a lie. The deepest punishment of a lie is—the liar. He has to live with a man he cannot trust. That is an uneasy hell.

—The Way

Sin and the body are not made for each other—they are allergic to each other.

—Song of Ascents

The idea that sin is natural and goodness unnatural is foreign to the Christian faith.

—Song of Ascents

It is impossible that the wrong thing should have a right result in the long run.

—The Way

Nothing is more beautiful than righteousness; nothing is more hideous than self-righteousness.

—The Christ of the Mount

The only way to keep evil going is to throw enough good around it to keep it going.

—Song of Ascents

Swearing isn't the sign of a he-man; it is the sign of a weak man; and the more he swears the weaker he is.

—The Way

Two evils never make a good.

—The Way

Most of us are the bellhops of our appetites.

—The Christ of the Mount

Quacks treat symptoms; doctors treat diseases. Condemnation is a symptom; sin is the disease.

—In Christ

The "new morality" is nothing more and nothing other than the old immorality demanding acceptance and public approval.

—Song of Ascents

"He went away sorrowful" is the history of every single person who gives up Christ for something else.

—Growing Spiritually

Is it hard to be a Christian? No, it is hard not to be a Christian.

—Song of Ascents

Evil is the Great Illusion: God is the Great Illumination.

—The Way

The pay-off determines the worth.

—Growing Spiritually

As poison is to the blood, as ugliness is to the eye, as hate is to the heart, so sin is to me.

—In Christ

Inward division is the basis of the modern misery.

—Victory Through Surrender

The ultimate question about any man's character is: Are there any circumstances under which that man will lie? If so, he has a worm eating at his heart.

—The Way

You cannot take His power and His creative "rest" unless you take His morality as your working code.

—Song of Ascents

All evil is a parasite on the good.

—Growing Spiritually

If the center of s-i-n is the big "I," then the center of deliverance from sin is the deliverance from the "I".

—Growing Spiritually

You are dead to sin to the degree that you are alive to God.

—In Christ

Evil is alien—it is not food; the system cannot digest it.

—The Way

They lived on a prejudice and died of a jaundice.

—The Christ of the Mount

Innate depravity is the self surrendered to nothing but itself—the self become God.

—Song of Ascents

When I break with God I break with life.

—The Way

Worry is distrust, and distrust is sin.

—The Christ of the Mount

Anything that leaves you at the center is off-center.

—Song of Ascents

If He doesn't save us from sin He doesn't save us from anything—including hell. For sin is hell begun.

—In Christ

He who spits against the wind spits in his own face.

—The Way

If we won't live with Christ, we can't live with ourselves.

—*Song of Ascents*

Success

All you have to do is be true to the highest you know, and success and failure are in the hands of God. That emancipates you from the bondage to succeed.

—*The Way*

Suffering

You can decide whether it will make you bitter or better.

—*Growing Spiritually*

Antioch Christians: The persecution persecuted them into productivity. It cost something to be a Christian and it meant something.

—*The Reconstruction of the Church*

Adverse winds can blow you forward if you know how to manipulate the sails.

—*The Way*

The crushed violet perfumes the heel that crushes it.

—*The Way*

Temptation

Temptation knocked at my door; I asked Christ to answer, and no one was there.

—*The Way*

Don't take hold of a thing unless you want that thing to take hold of you. You destine yourself to the deed when you decide to approach it.

—*The Way*

Those who think they can indulge at the place of seeing and can pull back in the place of seeking, are putting their feet on a slippery bank. . . . In temptation flight is better than fight.

—*The Way*

You see, then seek. For seeing creates desire and desire creates emotion, and in the battle between the emotion and the will the emotion nearly always wins.

—*The Way*

Unity of Believers

If you belong to Christ and I belong to Christ we belong to each other.

—*Song of Ascents*

Our faith, and therefore our unity, are not in bishops, and not in baptism, but in Christ. The only place we can be united is in Christ, for in Him we are one.

—In Christ

This unity in Christ is not a unity of uniformity, but unity in diversity.

—In Christ

Here we enter into a fellowship; sometimes we will agree to differ; always we will resolve to love and unite to serve.

—Sat Tal Ashram wall mottoes

When there is heart agreement in loyalty to Christ, we can put up with a lot of lesser disagreements.

—In Christ

Christ and Christ alone is the issue. He is the Dividing Line. If we are in Him nothing else need divide us.

—The Way

The "Hallelujah Chorus" must be a chorus and not a solo.

—Song of Ascents

There is no such thing as being in Christ unrelated to others who are in Christ.

—In Christ

Not what I believe, but Whom!

—In Christ

Everybody who belongs to Christ belongs to everybody who belongs to Christ.

—In Christ

VICTORIOUS LIVING

Surrendered to Christ you are master of everything.

—Song of Ascents

Don't bear trouble, use it. . . . Don't explain evil; exploit it; make it serve you.

—Song of Ascents

Where there is God's will, there is a way.

—The Way

The Christian is incorrigible. If life hands him a lemon, he adds some sugar and makes it into lemonade.

—Growing Spiritually

Stephen in his fall, raised up Saul. Which won, stones or spirit? The stones are now scattered stones on a Palestinian roadside. The spirit of Stephen marches deathless through the ages.

—The Way

When we can sing in the face of death, we can sing in the face of everything.

—*Growing Spiritually*

When you can make the devil serve you, then you are victorious. . . . Make everything kick you forward.

—*Song of Ascents*

I have hold of something that nothing can hold! It conquers everything!

—*The Way*

[Stephen] His eyes were in focus—the Throne was at the center and the trouble was on the margin.

—*The Way*

The Christian way has a way now, and it is the way where life is adequate, victorious, effective, and happy now—apart from immortality.

Have a funeral service and bury your old dead words and attitudes and put a "No Resurrection" sign over them.

—*Growing Spiritually*

The life of victory is normal Christianity. The Holy Spirit has taken possession of the subconscious mind, has cleansed, redirected, and dedicated the three driving urges of self, sex, and the herd. Those urges are still there, for the person is not depersonalized. The self is there, but no longer the center, no longer controlling life. The self is a Spirit-controlled self. Sex is still there, but no longer at the center, controlling the rest of life. The life is not sex-controlled, but Spirit-controlled. The herd urge is still there, but no longer fastened upon such entities as class or race or nation as supreme loyalties. Now it is fastened upon the Kingdom of God as the supreme loyalty. . . . So now conscious mind and subconscious mind are under one sway and control.

—*The Way*

When I fall, I fall on my knees; when I stumble, I stumble into His arms.

—*Song of Ascents*

As long as you remain in Christ you possess all the strength, all the goodness, all the victory, all the love of Christ. You are therefore invincible.

—*In Christ*

Character is destiny.

—*The Christ of the Mount*

WAR

War is a worm-eaten god.

—*The Way*

International anarchy is the cause of international war.

—*The Way*

In war the end is not a tribunal of right but a tribunal of might. Police force and force used in war are different.

—*The Way*

Why should we burn down the house of civilization periodically to get rid of a few rats? Can't we build a house of civilization that is ratproof?

—*The Way*

War is an attempt to act like the devil in order to get the devil out of people. It cannot be done.

—*The Christ of the Mount*

Two patterns for peace are emerging: (1) Leagues, pacts, treaties, charters among sovereign nations. (2) A federal union of the world.

—*The Way*

If the Way is right, then war is wrong.

—*The Way*

"A war to end war" is the supreme moral absurdity.

—*The Christ of the Mount*

You don't have to submit to a wrong or an evil system, and you don't have to go to war; there is an alternative to both—nonviolent noncooperation.

—*Song of Ascents*

Getting rid of evil by evil means you infect yourself with the very evil you try to get rid of.

—*The Way*

If war is right, Christ is inherently wrong. If Christ is right, war is inherently wrong.

—*The Way*

WORTH OF PERSONS

The Son of Man is for the sons of men.

—*The Reconstruction of the Church*

Whenever Christ touches life, that life takes on significance, the nobodies become somebodies.

—*The Way*

His way is the way that looks upon every person as "a man for whom Christ died."

—*Song of Ascents*

What you can give, and what is in the hands of a democratic society to give, is equality of opportunity. That is the birthright of every man born under a democracy.

—*Song of Ascents*

Jesus did not use words ending in "ity," which we are so fond of using. He did not talk about personality, He talked of persons. He did not ask us to love humanity, He asked us to love people. It costs little to enthuse about love of humanity, for it is so vague and abstract that it demands nothing but sentiment.

—*The Christ of the Mount*

We are all equal before God, therefore equal before men.

—*The Reconstruction of the Church*

Peter never became a world evangelist; he was caught in a racialism and never quite got free.

—*The Way*

The segregationists will only segregate themselves.

—*The Reconstruction of the Church*

All races have considered themselves superior. . . . We laugh, but it has been no laughing matter in history.

—*Song of Ascents*

I would rather choose irreligious humanism than inhuman religion.

—*The Christ of the Mount*

You cannot give equality in character of achievement to the white man or to the Negro. That must be earned by character and achievement.

—*Song of Ascents*

Jesus met each man and each moment as if the whole of eternity were concentrated in that man in that moment. And it was!

—*The Christ of the Mount*

We have been in an alien land of racialism, now we will be at home in the Kingdom.

—*The Reconstruction of the Church*

If you lose Christ you lose the humanitarian, and if you lose the humanitarian you lose Christ.

—*The Reconstruction of the Church*

To exclude a brother in Christ is to exclude Christ.

—*In Christ*

Every person is infinitely precious in the sight of God and must be in the sight of men.

—*Growing Spiritually*

The reconstructed church must be a society of one class—the class of those "for whom Christ died." If it is other than that it is other than Christian.

—*The Reconstruction of the Church*

No man can be permanently raised while any man is permanently degraded. We are bound up together.

—*The Christ of the Mount*

The Church must have a passion for souls, but it must also have a passion for people—soul, mind, and body. For it is possible to love people's souls and be unconcerned about what happens to their bodies, their minds, their dwellings, their environment.

—*The Way*

Everybody is your neighbor—literally everybody!

—*Growing Spiritually*

Sayings Attributed to E. Stanley Jones

Life with Christ is an endless hope; without Him a hopeless end.

Fixed in Christ, and flexible in everything else.

The church is a subject of salvation, not the source of it.

The greatest medicine for health is conversion. The greatest tonic for toning up the whole system is the Holy Spirit.

What is the difference between good intentions and a crying baby in a church service? None. Both should be carried out immediately.

If you belong to Christ, and I belong to Christ, then we belong to each other.

Topical Index